Books by
Edith M. Patch

NATURE STUDY

Dame Bug and Her Babies

Hexapod Stories

Bird Stories

First Lessons in Nature Study

Holiday Pond

Holiday Meadow

Holiday Hill

Holiday Shore

Mountain Neighbors

Desert Neighbors

Forest Neighbors

Prairie Neighbors

NATURE AND SCIENCE READERS

Hunting

Outdoor Visits

Surprises

Through Four Seasons

Science at Home

The Work of Scientists

SURPRISES

SURPRISES

by

Edith M. Patch
and Harrison E. Howe

illustrated by

Eleanor G. Eadie

YESTERDAY'S CLASSICS

ITHACA, NEW YORK

This edition, first published in 2022 by Yesterday's Classics, an imprint of Yesterday's Classics, LLC, is an unabridged republication of the text originally published by the Macmillan Company in 1933. For the complete listing of the books that are published by Yesterday's Classics, please visit www.yesterdaysclassics.com. Yesterday's Classics is the publishing arm of Gateway to the Classics which presents the complete text of hundreds of classic books for children at www.gatewaytotheclassics.com.

ISBN: 978-1-63334-184-5

Yesterday's Classics, LLC
PO Box 339
Ithaca, NY 14851

CHAPTERS AND GAMES IN THIS BOOK

A LETTER TO THE BOYS AND GIRLS

Dear Boys and Girls:

There are thirty-nine chapters in this book. Besides these chapters, there are many science games.

Sometimes people who write books for children tell them how to study the books. We think you will not need to be told. We think, when one of you reads a chapter, you will say, "Now I shall try to see for myself everything this chapter tells about." And when you have read about the science games, we think you will play as many of them as you can.

In this book we have told you as many interesting facts as there seemed to be room for in thirty-nine chapters. Every fact may surprise you when you first learn about it. You may say, "I never knew why the cotton plant needs fibers to use!" after you read the chapter that begins on page 1. Perhaps you will say, "I never guessed that spider silk could be made into cloth!" after you have read page 37.

Here is something for you to remember. All the facts and surprises in this book are outside the book, too. Of course they had to be in the world outside before they could be found and put into a book.

Perhaps, by the time you have read all the chapters and played all the science games, you will have a very good habit. You may have the habit of looking at things in the world outside books and trying to learn about them, too. But perhaps you have that habit already. Many boys and girls have.

So, instead of telling you how to study these chapters, we shall just wish you many good science hunts, both inside this book and outside it. We hope, too, you may have many pleasant surprises.

Your friends,

EDITH M. PATCH

HARRISON E. HOWE

A SUMMER DRESS

1. Cotton Fibers

Before Ruth could have her every-day dress to wear, it had to be cut from cloth and sewed.

Before the cloth could be cut and sewed, it had to be woven from threads.

Before the threads could be woven into cloth, they had to be spun from fibers.

And before the fibers could be spun into threads, they had to grow on cotton plants.

So Ruth liked to say, "Once upon a time this cotton dress was growing on some plants."

The cotton plants, of course, had no need of dresses. They had other uses for their fibers.

Dandelion seeds with fibers

Did you ever see a dandelion plant after the yellow blossom head had grown into a white seed head? Did you blow some of the seeds with your breath and watch them move away in the air?

Did you ever find a milkweed plant when the seed pods were ripe and open? Did you notice how the seeds

Milkweed seeds with fibers

came out of the pods and sailed far out of sight with the wind?

Dandelions and milkweeds and many other plants have seeds with little fine fibers on them. The fibers act like tiny sails. With the help of these sails, the seeds travel in the air for a while. In that way they go to new places before they settle down and start to grow.

Cotton seeds with fibers

Can you think, now, what use a cotton plant may have for its fine white fibers?

If you guess that the fibers are sails for their seeds, you will be right.

Cotton seeds grow in pods. There are many seeds in one pod. The pods open when the seeds are ripe. Then the fluffy fibers are taken into the air by the wind and go off with the seeds that are hitched to them.

There was a time when people did not know how to make cloth with cotton fibers. In those days all the cotton plants grew in hot countries.

In such places cotton plants live from year to year. Some kinds grow to be trees or large shrubs. There is no cold weather to kill them.

But long ago people learned how to use cotton fibers. Then men living in cooler countries obtained seeds and grew these useful plants.

In cooler places, however, cotton cannot live in winter. So the seeds must be planted each year.

There are many places in the southern part of the United States where cotton can grow in summer. The summer is so long that the plants can grow and blossom and have ripe seeds each year.

But in the North the summers are too short for the seeds of these plants to ripen.

Ruth said, "If I lived in the South, perhaps I could see just how the cotton looks before it is spun into threads and made into cloth."

Cotton plant

2. Blue Dye

Cotton fibers are white and Ruth's cotton dress was blue. So Ruth knew that the cloth had been dyed. But she did not know where the dye came from. Do you?

The name of the blue dye is indigo. There are different kinds of plants from which this blue color can be taken. They grow in many countries.

But the indigo plants from which most blue dye has been made grow in India. There was a time when indigo plants grew on more than a million acres of land in India.

Do you know how a pea plant looks? Have you seen what sort of leaves and flowers and seed pods it has?

Did you ever see sweet peas growing? Did you notice the leaves and the pods that held the little pea-like seeds?

Indigo plants have leaves shaped somewhat like those of sweet-pea plants. Their seeds grow in much the same sort of pods. Their blossoms, though much smaller, have somewhat the same shape.

There is a good reason why peas and sweet peas and indigo plants should have leaves and flowers and seed pods that are somewhat alike. They all belong to the same family of plants.

At first the people of India had no machinery to help them make

A beating vat

10

indigo dye. They cut the plants by hand with knives. Then they put them into great vats. There the plants were covered with water.

Later the men let the water and plant juice run into lower vats, called beating vats. The men stood in the vats and beat the liquid with paddles. This was the way they mixed air with the liquid.

There was more blue color in the liquid after it was beaten and mixed with air. It colored the legs of the men who were working in the vats.

After a while the indigo coloring stuff sank to the bottom of the vats. Then it was taken and dried and made into little cakes of dye.

Ruth's grandmother and her grandmother's mother had had blue cotton dresses. These dresses were dyed with indigo that came from indigo plants. In those days that was the best kind of blue dye.

But, now, people can get dye in a different way. They have learned how to make indigo in factories. When they do this they start with coal tar.

Coal tar is black. It is thicker and stickier than molasses. It has a very bad smell. It is a poison.

Many useful things are made from this ugly, black, sticky poison.

Men boil the coal tar and change it in different ways. And after a while it is not coal tar any more. It has been changed so that it is something else.

Fragrant perfumes and certain good-tasting harmless flavors are made from coal tar. Beautiful dyes are made from it, too. And some of these dyes are blue indigo.

The indigo from coal tar that was used to dye Ruth's dress gave it a lovely color. It was, indeed, lovelier than the indigo blue in her grandmother's dress.

For men can make more shades of blue, now, than they could a long time ago. So Ruth could choose the dark shade or the light shade that she liked best of all.

3. Button, Button

Who has the button? Well, Ruth has it now. It is the large pretty white one on the belt of her blue dress.

Once, however, it belonged to a little animal that lived in the muddy bed of a big river. Of course it was not a button, then. It was a part of the animal's shell. This animal that lived in the river mud was a mussel.

Mussels are related to oysters and clams. The bodies of these animals are nearly alike.

Each of these animals has a shell in two halves. There is a hinge at one edge of the halves. So the shell can open and shut.

Fresh-water mussels

The mussel opens its shell a little when it breathes. Water gets inside the open shell. There is some air in the water that the mussel breathes. This animal has a breathing tube in its body and the water runs through the tube.

A clam or an oyster or a mussel has only one foot, as a snail has. It is shaped a little like your tongue. You can open your mouth and stick out your tongue. And a mussel can open its shell and push out its foot.

Such a foot acts much like a little plow. It can be shoved through the mud ahead of the shell. So that makes it easy for the mussel to move its shell through the mud, too.

Mussel shells are dark and rather rough outside. But inside they are smooth and shiny. They are nearly white, though they often have lovely tints of very pale colors.

Animals like mussels and clams and oysters make their own shells. The shells are small while the animals are young and tiny. The animals grow bigger and they make their shells bigger, too. So their shells are always large enough to cover them.

The beautiful smooth pale lining of such a shell is called mother-of-pearl. That is a good name for it because it is made of the same sort of stuff as a pearl. But a pearl is small and is not fastened to the shell.

Many of the animals that can make mother-of-pearl to line their shells can make pearls, too.

Sometimes a grain of sand gets inside a mussel's shell and hurts the mussel. Its body is comfortable only when it touches smooth things.

So what does the mussel's body do with the hard scratching grain of sand? It makes a smooth round pearl to cover it. The sand is in the middle of the pearl. The smooth pearl does not hurt the soft body of the mussel.

Pearls can be used for beads. Mother-of-pearl shells can be cut into different shapes and used for buttons and knife handles and other things.

So people catch these animals for their shells and hunt for pearls.

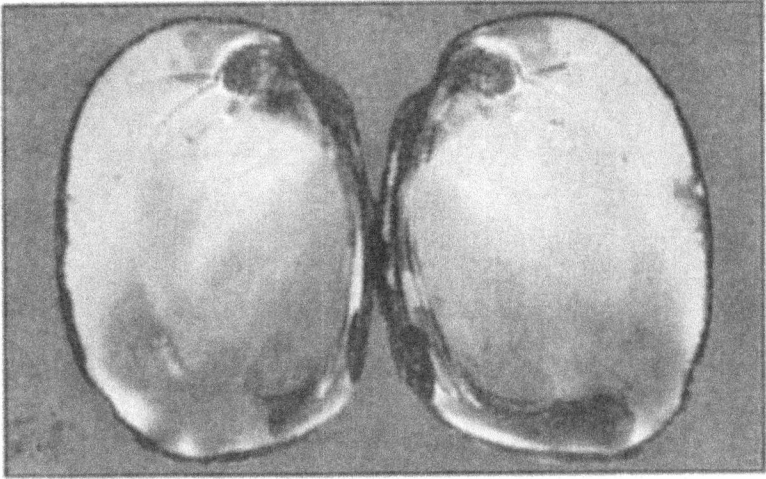

Shells lined with mother-of-pearl

Some kinds of animals that make mother-of-pearl and pearls live in salt sea water. Others live in rivers and ponds. The kind that had Ruth's button first and lived in the muddy bed of a river was called a freshwater mussel.

4. Starch

Ruth liked to have her cotton dress starched every time it was washed. Not enough to make it too stiff! Just enough to make it seem fresh!

The starch came from the store in hard dry white lumps. The lumps could be crushed into fine powder.

A little starch was put into water and boiled until it was a sticky paste. More boiling water was added until the starch paste was thin enough. Then Ruth's dress was dipped into it and dried and ironed.

One day Ruth said: "Mother, a plant made the fibers in my cotton dress. An animal made the

Corn seeds have starch in them.

mother-of-pearl in my button. The color came from coal tar. Where did the starch come from?"

So her mother told her about starch.

Plants make starch. They use it for food. It is the most common food they use when they start to grow.

Many kinds of plants store up starch food in their thick parts.

The thick bulbs of lily plants have a great deal of starch in them. It is ready to use for food when the lilies start to grow in the spring.

Potatoes have much starch. If you cut a potato in thin slices and leave it in a dish of cold water, you can find some starch in the bottom of the dish in a few hours.

Most plants put starch into their seeds. Then the baby plants have the right food when they start to grow.

Animals cannot make starch in their own bodies. But they can get it for food when they eat certain parts of plants.

People get starch to eat in potatoes and bananas and Hubbard squash. We get it in foods made from seeds like rice and wheat and oats and corn.

We use more starch for food than in other ways. But we have many other uses for it, too. And one of our uses for starch is to make some kinds of cloth stiff with it. Such starched cloth does not soil so easily as cloth that has not been starched.

Field of Indian corn, or maize

Rice starch is sometimes used for very fine thin clothes.

Most starch that is taken from potatoes is sent to factories. It is used to stiffen new cloth.

Wheat starch is used in many laundries. Cloth bends easily when it is stiffened with this kind of starch.

Corn starch is also good and it is cheap. This kind is used a great deal for starching clothes.

The corn plant stores starch in its seeds. The seeds are the kernels that grow on the corn cob. A kernel is more than half starch.

"The next time I see a corn plant growing," said Ruth, "I shall thank it for laundry starch."

SCIENCE GAMES

1. Three Puzzles

I have fine fibers on my seed.
Men take my fibers when they need
To make white thread or cloth to sell.
What boy or girl my name can tell?

Before men learned to be so wise,
They did not make gay coal tar dyes;
But colored with my juice so blue.
You know my name? I think you do!

My pretty seeds, in even row,
Upon a cob they always grow.
My starch is used for many a dress.
My name is easy, now, to guess!

2. Pictures

1. Draw a picture of a shell that is lined with mother-of-pearl. Show the two halves of the shell. Show where the hinge is.

2. Draw pictures of things that can be made from mother-of-pearl.

3. Read the last four lines that you find on this page. Then write these four lines on a piece of paper and draw a picture of an animal to go with them. Put the animal's name under the picture.

I have one foot and only one.
I plow through mud. I cannot run.
I have a very lovely shell.
My name? I think you know it well!

3. Questions to Answer

1. Is there more warm weather in the northern part of the United States than in the southern part?

2. What sort of weather does a cotton plant need?

3. Do people raise corn in the state where you live? Do they raise potatoes there? (If you do not know how to answer the questions about potatoes and corn, ask some older person to tell you.)

4. Can you name three kinds of seeds that have fibers on them? How do seeds use these fibers?

5. If you wished to have some relatives of indigo plants in your garden, what seeds would you plant?

4. Starch Gardens

Plant some seeds of corn, wheat, and rice in a school garden or a home garden, if you can.

If you have no garden to use, plant some of these seeds in tin cans (with holes in the bottoms) or in flower-pots. They will grow for a while in cans or pots.

What food is there in these seeds for the young plants to use?

Ask some one how to cut a potato in pieces to be planted. Plant some pieces in a garden or a can or a pot.

What food is there in old potatoes for young potato plants to use when they start to grow?

SILK AND LINEN

1. Ruth's Silk Scarf

Ruth chose her own scarf. Her father went to the store with her. He told her to buy the one she liked best.

"I'll take the pretty silk one, please," she said. "I've never had a caterpillar scarf before!"

Of course "a caterpillar scarf" was a funny name for it. But it was rather a good name even if it was funny. For some caterpillars really did make all the silk fibers there were in the scarf.

Such caterpillars are called silkworms. They make the fibers for their own cocoons.

Silkworms, cocoons, and moths

31

Then people unwind the fibers from the cocoons and make cloth with them.

A silkworm hatches from an egg that one kind of moth lays. People keep moths of this kind for the eggs they lay. Caterpillars hatch from the eggs and grow until they are old enough to spin their silk cocoons.

These insects have been cared for in China for many, many years. One name for them is Chinese Silkworm.

At first all the silk cloth in the world was made in China. No one anywhere else knew how to get the fibers for this kind of cloth. This was a secret that the Chinese people did not tell.

Men in other parts of the world

thought that, perhaps, silk fibers grew on plants, as some other kinds of fibers do. So they hunted for plants with silk fibers but they never found any.

There is an old story about two men who went to China and learned the secret of silk. They saw how the moths were cared for until they laid their eggs. They found out how to keep the eggs. They watched to see how to feed the caterpillars while they were growing. They learned, too, how to put the silk cocoons into hot water so that the fibers would unwind without breaking.

Then these men took some of the eggs and carried them into another country. That was a long while ago.

Mulberry leaves and fruit

Now silkworms are kept in different countries. They can live in any place where mulberry trees can grow. These caterpillars eat mulberry leaves. So one name for them is Mulberry Silkworm.

Inside a silkworm's body are two little parts that can make silk. These two parts are called silk glands. The caterpillar pushes the silk out of the glands into two tubes. These tubes come together near an opening in the caterpillar's lower lip.

The silk is not a fiber while it is in the glands. It is a sort of sticky liquid then. But it hardens into a fiber as soon as it comes out of the opening in the caterpillar's lip. The air changes it from a liquid to a fiber.

Many other caterpillars, besides mulberry silkworms, spin silk cocoons. The fibers of most of these cocoons are not suitable for men to use for silk cloth. But some of them are.

One of the caterpillars that eats oak leaves spins good strong fibers. These fibers are used in making the cloth that is called pongee silk.

Some other animals, besides insects, have silk glands. Perhaps you have watched spiders spin their silk webs.

There is an island far away in the warm Indian Ocean where men take care of spiders for the silk they spin. They put their pet spiders in little stalls and take the fibers as fast as they are made.

The fibers from a number of spiders are caught together on a little tool and twisted into a thread. Soft and beautiful cloth is made from such spider silk.

This kind of spider makes strong silk.

Cloth from spider silk, indeed, may be stronger than that made from silk of silkworms. But cloth from spider silk is not so common and it costs much more.

So Ruth was right when she called her scarf a caterpillar scarf instead of a spider scarf!

2. Robert's Linen Handkerchiefs

Robert went to a store to buy handkerchiefs.

Some were colored and some were white. Some were cotton and some were linen and some were silk.

He knew about the fibers in cotton handkerchiefs. And he had heard where silk fibers come from. But no one had ever told him about linen fibers.

At last he bought two handker-chiefs and took them home to show to his mother. "I chose the linen kind," he said, "because I thought you might like to tell me a story about them. Do plants or animals make linen fibers?"

Then Robert and his mother laughed. They both thought it was funny to buy handkerchiefs just to hear stories about them.

Flax plants have slender stems.

The fibers from which linen cloth is made grow in flax plants. They are not light fluffy fibers growing on the seeds. Flax seeds have no fibers for sails. They do not travel in the air.

Flax does not need a very long warm season. It can thrive in almost any climate that has about one hundred warm days in summer. That allows plenty of time for a flax plant to grow from a seed and have seeds of its own.

A flax plant has a stem from one foot to four feet high. Its branches are slender; its leaves are small and narrow. Its flowers are bright blue.

Years ago almost every farmer in this country grew some flax on his own land.

When the fiber was ready to use, the farmer's wife and daughters spun it into linen yarn. The women wove the linen yarn into cloth for clothes and sheets and tablecloths and towels and handkerchiefs and napkins and other things they needed to use.

A field of flax in blossom

In those days people made cloth for themselves in their own homes. Now linen and other cloth is made in factories and can be bought in stores.

So, now, flax is grown in large fields and the fiber is sent to factories. It is not grown in so many little fields on nearly every farm.

But people would miss the flax flowers if they could not see them. So they often have a few flax plants growing in their flower gardens.

Linen fiber is in the stem of a flax plant. It is in one layer of the bark.

The fiber cannot be taken out easily unless the stem is soaked in water until it becomes soft. While it is soaking it becomes changed in certain ways. This is called rotting, or retting, the flax.

Sometimes flax is retted by leaving the stems lying in a wet field where they will be kept damp by the dew. A better way is to let the flax soak in a pool or in a slow stream of water.

Taking the flax stems out of the water

After the stems have been retted, the fibers are separated from the other parts of the flax stems by machinery.

The best fibers are used for cloth. Some of the coarse, poor fibers are made into rope and string. Some are used for stuffing cushions and furniture.

Linen is not a new kind of cloth. It is the very oldest kind made from plant fibers that we know about. It has been made for thousands of years.

Flax was grown in Egypt long ago when a man named Moses lived there. In the old days the princes of Egypt wore linen robes.

Robert liked to hear some of the old stories about men who wore strange linen clothes.

His mother told him how the princes of Egypt made gifts of linen clothes to people they liked.

Pharaoh and Joseph

She read him a story about Pharaoh and Joseph. "And Pharaoh took off his ring from his hand, and put it upon Joseph's hand, and arrayed him in fine linen, and put a gold chain about his neck."

SCIENCE GAMES

1. Hunting for Fibers

1. Hunt for a place where milk-weeds grow. Find some old dry gray broken milkweed stems. Pull the long thread-like fibers away from the outside of the stems. Do you think an oriole would like such fibers to weave into its nest? See if they are strong enough to braid. Can you weave them into a little mat for a doll's house?

2. Do you know some one who has flax plants growing in a field or a garden? If you do, ask if you may have a stem of flax. Soak the stem in water until you can get the linen fibers to use.

3. If you do not find flax or milkweed, use other plant fibers. Try old brown grass or hay. If the stems break when they are dry, soak them in water for a little while.

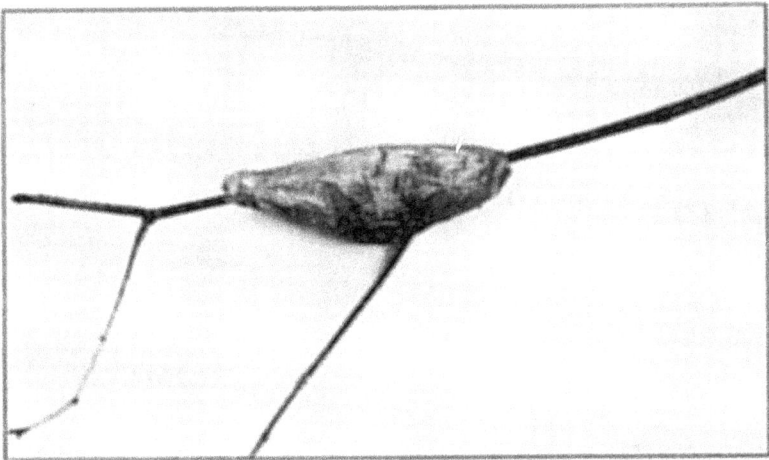

You may find a cocoon like this.

4. Hunt for an old cocoon. If the cocoon is empty, put it into boiling water. Then see if you can unwind some fibers to twist into a silk thread.

47

2. Choose the Right Word

Here is a story with six words left out of it. And here are the six words.

moths   fibers   mulberry

silk   cocoons   caterpillars

Copy this story on a piece of paper and put the words in the right places.

Long ago some people in China had a secret. They knew how to make ****. Some men went to China and watched the Chinese taking care of some pet ****. These pets were fed with **** leaves. The pets spun ****. The men saw how the Chinese unwound the ****. The pets hatched from eggs that were laid by ****. So the men took some of these eggs to other countries.

A WINTER COAT

1. The Color of the Coat

The first fall days had been warm. Thin clothes had been comfortable, then. But those days were over for the year. It was late fall, now, and almost as cold as early winter.

Robert and his playmates were wearing coats to school. To be sure, they did not need coats while they were running fast. They often took them off when they were at play.

Sometimes Robert asked his mother: "May I leave my coat at home? I need to take it off when I run and play. It is just in the way most of the time!"

But such teasing was useless. Mother was certain that the time had come for warm clothes. So she said, "Be sure to wear your red coat to-day."

And whenever Robert stood waiting at a corner where a sharp wind came whirling around him, he was glad he had his coat on. At such times he even buttoned it up to the collar.

One day, in the school yard, Robert looked at the coats all the boys were wearing. There were blue coats, brown coats, gray coats, and several red coats like his own. He thought the red coats looked warmest of all. They seemed very cozy for a chilly day. He wondered if some colors really made cloth warmer than others.

After he thought about cloth and colors for a while, he asked his father some questions.

Robert's father told him that color itself adds no warmth to cloth. But, strange as it may seem, some colors make us think of heat and some make us think of cold.

Sky blue or pale green or most light colors, or white, usually make us think of cool things or places. So, perhaps, we feel cooler when we look at them. Clothes of such colors seem more pleasant in summer than in winter.

Red, or dark shades of any color, or black, help us think of warmth. A red coat looks warm and that makes it seem more comfortable in winter.

Although color itself does not really make cloth cold or warm, some colors become warmer in sunshine than other colors. That is because certain colors hold heat from sunshine more than other colors do. Dark colors and black hold such heat more than light colors and white.

So if you have on even very thin black clothes in summer, you can be comfortable only in shady places. If you wear them in the sunshine in the middle of some summer day, you will begin to suffer in a very short time.

Now what do you think really kept Robert warm in his coat? If the color did not make him warm, do you think it was the cloth?

2. The Cloth of the Coat

Some clothes are made of silk. Many boys and girls in China and Japan have silk coats. But such coats would not be warm enough for a winter day where Robert lived. His snug red coat was not made of silk fibers.

Many clothes are made of cotton. People in India and other warm countries use cotton more than any other fiber. They choose it because it is cheap and because they can keep cool in cotton. But Robert's winter coat was not a cotton one.

Neither was it made of linen. For linen fibers are even less suitable for cold weather than silk and cotton.

Of what was that coat made, if it was not silk or cotton or linen?

Why, wool of course! Perhaps you guessed that the bright red winter coat was a woolen one. But do you know why wool fibers keep you warmer than other kinds? Robert did not know. So he asked his father.

Wool is the hair of sheep. Each hair, or fiber, has many tiny scales on it. These scales are so small that you cannot see them unless you look at them through a microscope. (The curved glasses in a microscope make small things look large.)

The little scales on one hair catch into those of other hairs, when the wool is spun into yarn. In this way the fibers of wool are easily tangled together and each tangled place is like a very little pocket filled with air.

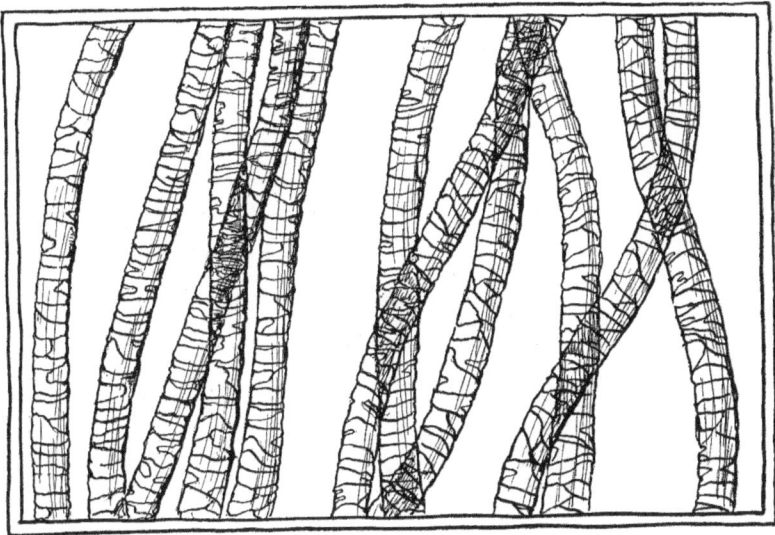

Wool fibers have little scales on them.

Of course there are thousands and thousands of such little pockets in even a small piece of woolen cloth. And each tiny pocket is filled with quiet air.

Now a layer of quiet air is the best thing to keep warmth or cold from passing. When Robert had his wool coat on, the warmth of his body could not pass out and the cold could not pass in at all easily.

So you see Robert's red wool coat, itself, was not warm. He was warm inside it because the quiet air in the many, many pockets in the wool fibers kept the heat from his body from getting away quickly. The coat helped him to keep himself warm.

Robert had one more question to ask. He said, "Father, if other fibers had good places to hold air, would other kinds of coats keep me warm, too?"

"Yes, they would," said his father.

A lamb wears a coat of woolen hairs.

Then he told Robert how cotton is sometimes combed to make fluffy cotton blankets and fleecy underclothes. Such cotton cloth can hold quiet air in the fluffy places. It keeps warmth in and cold out much better than smooth cotton.

But cotton or silk or linen fibers are not covered with tiny scales. They cannot be tangled into little air pockets that stay as well as the pockets in wool fibers do.

Robert was glad to know the reason why his coat kept him so warm.

"You know," he said, "it is fun to think of all the tiny air pockets this wool coat has in it. And red really is a jolly color to see in winter!"

SCIENCE GAMES

1. Quiet Air

You have read that a layer of quiet air keeps warmth or cold from passing.

You have learned that it is the quiet air held by wool fibers that makes a woolen coat a warm one to wear.

1. Ask some one to tell you why hot water stays hot in a thermos bottle.

2. When carpenters build houses, they leave places for quiet air to stay in the walls.

How does this help keep people warm in cold weather in the North?

How does it help keep people cool in hot weather in the South?

2. Color Rhymes

Here are the names of three colors.

red   green   white

Copy the lines on this page and put the name of each color in its place.

Summer and Winter Colors

When the summer sun shines hot on
    me,
I love the * * * * of a shady tree.

I like my clothes both thin and ****,
When the summer sun shines hot
    and bright.

But when 'tis very cold, instead,
There's nothing jollier than ****,
I like to see it much the same
As I like to watch a fire flame!

SOME FOOD
FROM PLANTS

1. Sugar

Animals need sugar for food. They get it from plants. Sugar is made by all plants that have green leaves. It is made in the green leaves when the sun shines on them.

Cows and horses get sugar when they eat green grass or dry hay. Insects get it when they eat the leaves or suck the juices of plants. Birds get it when they eat fruit.

After animals get sugar from plants there is some in their own bodies. So animals that eat meat get some sugar with their meat food.

But in the beginning the sugar must come from plants.

Some seeds are sweet. Sweet corn and green peas have sugar in them, as you can tell when they are in your mouth.

There is much sugar in some roots. Have you noticed that beets and carrots have a sweet taste?

You can tell that there is sugar in Hubbard squash and sweet potatoes, too.

Figs and dates and blueberries and pears and apples and bananas have sugar in them. What other fruits can you think of that taste sweet?

The sugar and syrup that people buy at stores are made from plants.

Green peas have sugar in them.

So you may thank plants for all the sweetness in candies and cookies and ice cream and cake.

Some plants have more sugar in them than others. Some have so much that people grow them so that they can get the sugar to use.

People grow sugar beets in great fields. These beets are not the pretty red tender beets we eat at the table. They are larger and have pale roots.

The roots are sent to a factory, where the sugar is taken out. The pulp that is left is fed to sheep and cattle. The beet leaves are not wasted, either. Sheep and cattle eat them, too.

All the sugar that is sold is not beet sugar. Some of it is cane sugar.

Children like to suck sugar-cane juice.

The sugar cane is a tall plant. It is related to Indian corn and it looks much like a giant corn stalk. Cane is a word that is sometimes used instead of stalk.

There is much more sugar in sugar cane than there is in corn stalks. When the cane is cut, it is taken to mills where the juice is pressed out. After the water is removed from the juice, the sugar is left.

You can visit fields of sugar cane in the South. It grows in warm places.

Sorgo is another sweet plant that is related to Indian corn and sugar cane. Sweet sorghum is another name for it. It can grow in the North as well as the South.

The juice of sorgo is pressed out in mills but it is not made into dry sugar. It is sold as syrup.

The sap of some trees is quite sweet. One kind of maple tree has such sweet sap that people take some of it to use.

Sap runs fastest in the early spring before the leaves grow. So men cut holes through the bark of sugar maple trees when the sap runs fast. Some of the sap runs out of the holes and is caught in pails that are fastened on the trees.

It is then poured into big kettles and boiled. The longer it boils the thicker it gets. First it is syrup and then, if it is boiled a much longer

Maple sugar is good to eat.

time, it is sugar. Some is sold as maple syrup and some as maple sugar.

Plants do not keep all their sugar in their leaves and roots and stalks or trunks. Many plants put their sweetest juices into their flowers. Such juice is called nectar.

People do not gather nectar and get syrup and sugar from it. They keep honey bees to work for them. The bees gather the nectar and make the honey and then people take some of the honey for themselves.

These insects work all through the warm weather getting the nectar and putting the honey into their honeycombs. They really get much more than they need. So people

Bees find sweet nectar in clover.

leave enough honey in the hive for the bees and take the rest for themselves.

The next time you eat some sweet food, you may feel glad that plants can make sugar while the sun is shining on their green leaves.

2. Seeds to Eat

Miss Lee asked the children in her room what kind of seeds they ate.

At first some of the boys and girls thought that was a funny question. One boy asked, "Do people eat seeds like birds?"

Miss Lee said: "People eat some of the very same kinds of seeds that birds like. Many birds like the seeds of the oat plant. How many of you ate oatmeal for breakfast this morning?"

The boys and girls who had oatmeal for breakfast raised their hands. Then all the children in the room tried to think of other kinds of seed food they ate.

Bobolinks like rice to eat. One name for them is ricebirds. Ruth said she liked rice pudding.

Miss Lee said, "Cracked wheat is a good food for chickens." Then the children talked about how wheat is ground into flour and how much bread and other food they had with wheat flour in it.

They talked about other kinds of bread, too. Some liked rye bread made with the ground seeds of the rye plant. Others liked bread and other food made from ground seeds of Indian corn.

People do not always eat butter on their bread. They often eat margarine instead.

Some margarine is made with oil that is pressed from cotton seeds. It is often made with oil from nuts and sometimes from animal fats.

Margarine is also used instead of lard in cooking. Some of the oil from cotton seeds is used for salad oil to eat with lettuce or fruit salads.

An important food is made for cows from cotton seeds after the oil is pressed out. It is called cottonseed meal.

One boy said he liked to eat peanut butter on his bread. Peanuts are seeds. They grow in pods as peas do.

The pods of garden peas and beans grow above ground. But there are some plants belonging to the same family that have underground pods.

Peanuts grow on the lower parts of the stems.

74

Peanut plants are related to peas and beans. Their pods grow underground.

Not all the seeds of peanut plants are roasted and eaten as nuts. Many are pressed like cotton seeds for the oil that is in them. Millions of gallons of peanut oil are used for food in the United States every year. Some of it is used in margarine.

After the oil is pressed out, the rest of the seed is put into peanut meal. Peanut meal is an excellent food for cows and pigs.

Many kinds of nuts that grow on trees are good seeds to eat. The children in Miss Lee's room named all the nuts they could remember.

What kind of seed foods do you like?

3. Juicy Fruits

Different important parts of flowering plants are called roots, stems, leaves, flowers, and fruits.

People who have learned most about plants say that fruits are the seeds and the parts that hold the seeds. They say that a fruit is a seed vessel.

So a pod of beans may be called the fruit of a bean plant, or a squash the fruit of a squash vine, or an orange the fruit of an orange tree, or a raspberry the fruit of a raspberry bush.

However, when we go to a store to buy beans and squashes we do not call them fruits. But we do call raspberries and oranges fruits.

So you see the word fruit is used in two ways. It is used in books about plants to mean the seed vessel of any flowering plant. And it is used in a common everyday way to mean certain seed vessels with good juicy pulp that we like to eat.

Watermelons are fruits that grow on long vines. These vines lie on the ground. The seed vessels in the flowers are very small at first but they grow until they are large and heavy. Some watermelons weigh more than seventy pounds when they are ripe.

Watermelon vines are related to squash and pumpkin and cucumber vines. They belong to the same plant family. This is the Gourd Family.

Plants that belong to the same family are similar in many ways. The flowers of melons and squashes and pumpkins and cucumbers have all much the same shape though they have not all the same size.

These plants need insects to carry the pollen from flower to flower. The seeds cannot grow without pollen. So when you see bees going in and out of melon blossoms you may thank these insects for the great pleasant fruits that grow on vines.

Many good-tasting fruits grow on plants that belong to the Rose Family.

The seed vessels of rose bushes are beautiful bright red shiny fruits called rose hips. There is not much pulp around the seeds in the hips of most kinds of roses. But some kinds have hips as large as small crab apples. People like to eat the pulpy part of such hips either raw or cooked.

Strawberry flowers and fruit

Some plants belonging to the Rose Family are short green plants with no tough woody stems. Strawberries are such plants.

Many kinds of plants that belong to this family are bushes. Two of these are raspberry and blackberry bushes. Another is the loganberry.

Blackberry flowers and fruit

But many plants of the Rose Family are bigger and stronger than bushes. They are trees. Some of the trees of this family have seed vessels with a number of seeds in the center, or core, like the apple and pear.

Some of them have fruits with but

one hard seed in each. Such seeds are called stones or pits. A cherry or a peach or a plum has a stone or pit in the center of the pulp.

Cherry flowers and fruit

A blackberry bush does not look like a cherry tree. A strawberry plant does not look like an apple or a plum tree. You may think it strange that all these fruits belong to the same plant family.

Perhaps, when you are older, you may like to study more about plants. You may like to study the plants of the Rose Family to see why people think they are related to one another. If you do, you will find that they are alike in many ways, even if they are so different in other ways.

You do not need to wait until you are older to learn about one likeness. You can learn about the flowers now. Find a blossom of an apple or a cherry or peach or plum or pear or strawberry or raspberry or blackberry. Look at it carefully to see if it is shaped very much like a little single rose blossom. How many petals does each of these flowers have?

Plants that belong to the Rose Family need insects to carry their pollen from flower to flower so that the seeds can grow. Many different kinds of bees help these plants in this way.

Did you ever thank some insects for the loveliest, sweetest cherry you ever ate? Did you ever think to say, "I thank you, little bees, for this good plum!"

Oranges and lemons and grapefruits come from trees that belong to the Rue Family. There are hundreds of kinds of plants that belong to this family. Many are shrubs or bushes and some are short plants with green stems.

Oranges and lemons and grape-fruits cannot live outdoors in the northern part of our country. Even in Florida and California and Texas they are sometimes injured by frost.

Orange flowers and fruit

There are other good juicy fruits that grow on plants belonging to other families. Perhaps you can name some that you like to eat.

4. Vegetables

Vegetable is a word that is used in more than one way. We may call any plant a vegetable. But we usually say vegetable when we speak of some part of a plant that we use for food.

We may eat any of the different parts of plants. So our vegetables may be leaves, stems, roots, flowers, seeds, or seed vessels.

Leaves of many plants are good to eat. Spinach and young beet leaves are cooked. Lettuce and cabbage leaves are eaten either raw or cooked.

Dandelion and chicory leaves are eaten raw if they have been grown in the dark so that their new leaves are tender and nearly white.

The green leaves of young dandelion plants which have been grown in the sunshine are good to eat, too, but they are usually cooked first.

A cabbage is a big thick bud. The stem inside a head of cabbage is so very short that the leaf buds are held close together. The only way they can grow is for the outer leaves to wrap around the inner leaves.

An onion is a kind of bud, too. We call this kind of bud a bulb. The new leaves in a bulb are thick. The outer leaf buds are wrapped around the inner leaf buds. Onions belong to the Lily Family.

You eat flowers when you eat cauliflower, just as you eat leaves when you eat cabbage. Cauliflower and cabbage belong to the same plant family, which is called the Mustard Family.

Turnips belong to the Mustard Family, too. Indeed turnips and cabbages and cauliflowers are so closely related that they all have the same first name in some plant books.

Sometimes plants that are closely related have much the same smell. Have you ever noticed that cabbages and cauliflowers and turnips smell alike when they are being cooked?

A turnip is not a head of flowers like a cauliflower. It is not a head of leaves like a cabbage. It is another thick part of a plant. The top of a turnip is the thickened part of a stem.

The rest of a turnip is the thickened part of a root.

Beets and carrots and parsnips and radishes are some other vegetables that are mostly thickened roots, though their tops are thickened stems.

A white potato is a thickened part of an underground stem. There are "eyes," or buds, in a potato. Branches with leaves can sprout from them.

Sweet potatoes are thickened roots and not thickened stems. Young stems with leaves and roots can sprout from them if they are kept in warm, moist sand. Then the young plants may be taken away and set out in a field to grow and have large thickened roots of their own.

Asparagus is a stem that many people like to eat. It is tender while it is so young that its branches and leaves have not yet grown.

The stems and leaves of milkweed are tender in the spring. They are good to eat when they are cooked. The tender young seed pods of milkweed are good to eat, too.

You already know about other seed vessels which we eat as vegetables, such as squash and cucumbers. And you know about such seeds as beans and peas and Indian corn, which we call vegetables.

What kind of vegetables do you think you would like to have for dinner to-day?

SCIENCE GAMES

1. A Grocery Party

Ask your teacher if you may have a grocery party at school.

1. Let one boy or girl be the grocer. This grocer will say, "I think I shall have in my store only foods that come from plants."

2. Let some of the boys and girls play they are people who grow good juicy fruits.

Take a piece of paper and make a list of juicy fruits that these growers might bring to sell to the grocer.

3. Let some of the children play they are people who grow vegetables. Make a list of different vegetables these growers might bring.

4. Let some girls and boys play they grow seeds of plants for food.

Make a list of different seeds these growers might bring to the grocer.

5. Ask the grocer to sell you a good root to eat. What could he sell you?

6. Ask the grocer to sell you some leaves that are good to eat. What do you think he would sell you?

7. Ask the grocer for food with starch in it. What foods do you know that have starch in them?

8. Perhaps you can think of other ways to plan a grocery party. Would you like to draw pictures of different vegetables for your grocery store?

2. Food Rhymes

Here are ten words. On these two pages is a place for each word.

Take a piece of paper and copy the lines from these two pages. Put each missing word in its right place.

beet	pea	plant	wheat
rose	rue	night	shell
bees	rice		

I bought some candy and it was sweet
With sugar from cane or sugar from
****.

Apples and pears, as every one knows,
Belong to the family of the ****.

The lemon and the orange, too,
Belong to the family of the ****.

Some cherry pollen was brought
by ****.
And cherries ripened on the cherry
trees.

A hard kind of pod is the peanut ****.
The seeds inside I like very well.

The peanut seed and the bean and
the ****,
They all break in halves, as you can see.

A potato tuber or a seed of ****.
Has starch in it that is good to eat.

The bobolinks are very fond of ****.
I like it, myself—in a pudding nice.

Plants make sugar if the sun is bright.
But they cannot do it in the ****.

I try to think of every kind of ****.
That gives me food, but I fear I can't!

FIRE STORIES

1. Fires with and without Matches

Most boys and girls like to make fires. But grown persons very often say, "Don't play with matches!" You may have heard mothers call, "Pour water on that fire!" to some children who had made one out-of-doors.

Of course fire is interesting. But it does not always do as you wish it would. And when it strikes you it hurts.

Many people suppose that things have always been as they see them. But perhaps you are like Robert. He wanted to know why and when and where and how.

How had fires been made when there were no matches? How do matches work? There are many questions to ask about fires.

Making a fire without matches

Before wood can burn it must, itself, be made hot. Boy Scouts learn how to make fires without matches. They use the same things that were used when no one had matches.

They turn a pointed stick against another piece of wood so fast that it becomes hot. After a while it grows so hot that it burns with a flame. Indians used to make fires this way.

Indians had another way of starting fires, too. They learned that when two very hard pieces of stone are struck together sparks fly. Stone which we call flint is hard enough to use in this way. Dry rotten wood may be set afire when it is held near such sparks.

When some things are mixed together they make a flame very easily. A match head does not need to be struck with flint to make it burn. Just scratching the match head makes it hot enough to burn.

The burning head makes the match stick so hot that it burns, too.

Now the heat from the match stick will make other small pieces of wood burn. The heat from these small burning pieces can make larger pieces so hot they begin to burn. Then, when such a wood fire is hot enough, coal can be heated on it until it is so very hot that it can burn. Coal must be much hotter than a match head before it will make a flame.

We are glad to have fire to give us heat when we are cold. It has many other uses, too.

A long time ago there were no airplanes or trains to carry letters swiftly. There were no telephones or other quick ways of telling people in far-off places what was happening. In those days men often used fires for signals.

They made fires on hills if they wished to let friends know that something important was happening. Then their friends could see the smoke in the daytime or the flames at night.

Men often use fire to show that they are happy. They may make a bonfire when something pleasant has happened. Or they may take torches and march in a parade.

Fire is used for the light it gives. There was a time when there was no other way to shut out the dark. People often used to read by the light of fires in fireplaces.

2. Things Cannot Burn without Air

Flames of fire may be of many colors, though most flames are yellow. They may have black edges. Sometimes there are little blue flames.

If you watch the different colors and shapes and motions of flames, you may think of names to give them. You may think of stories about what the flames seem to be doing. There are bright pictures to see in fires.

Fire may be given different colors by different things burning in the wood, the coal, or the oil.

When wood is in the ocean a long time, it becomes soaked with sea water. It is called driftwood because it drifts with the waves.

The waves bring some of the wood to the shore. Then people pick it up and put it in piles. It dries in the air, but salt and some other sea-water things remain in the wood even when it is dry.

The flames have different colors when such wood burns. Some of the colors come from the sea salt in the wood. Yellow is one of the colors. If you have no driftwood, you may like to throw a little table salt on other burning wood. The flames of this salt are yellow, only.

Nothing can burn well without plenty of air. A fire needs air while it burns as much as we need air when we breathe.

There is a gas in the air that we must have to keep us alive. This same gas is needed to make any fire.

If there is too little air, the fire is dull. That is why paper or wood or other things we wish to burn should not be piled so closely that the air cannot get through. Such a closely piled fire burns very slowly with few flames and much smoke. If the air is kept away still more, the fire goes out. But if some one stirs or pokes the slow-smoking fire, the air can get in and flames spring up from the hot wood.

We must pile sticks closely enough, but not too closely, if we are to have a good fire. The sticks must be near enough together so that each stick, as it burns, will heat another stick so hot that it can begin to burn, too. But there must always be room for air to keep the fire burning.

If we are careful with fire, it can help us in many ways and give us much pleasure. But if we are careless, it may do us many sorts of harm. It may spoil useful and beautiful things.

Fire causes great pain if it touches us. A little flame may be enough to start a fire that will grow big enough to burn down a whole house. A small camp fire may spread until it burns the trees in a forest for many miles.

A forest fire

So you need not be surprised when you hear grown persons say, "Don't play with matches!" And you will understand why mothers call, "Pour water on that fire!" when they see children making even a small one out-of-doors.

3. Candlelight

"I like the little fires that burn at the tops of candles," said Ruth. "I think candle flames are even prettier than the big flames of torches."

Ruth's mother heard her talking about candles and remembered what she said.

When Ruth was nine years old, her mother gave a birthday party for her. Ruth and her guests had a pleasant hour or so playing games. Then they were asked to come into the dining room.

When the doors to this room were opened, the faces of all the children looked glad. Yes, they knew they would have good things to eat at Ruth's party, but that was not the only reason they were happy. They were glad, too, because the room was so pretty.

The window curtains were down and the bright sunlight could not get in. The electric lights were not turned on. But the room was not dark. It was beautiful with candlelight.

Each candle was placed so that it was lovely to see. Its light made the things near it look lovely, too.

The smallest candles of all stood near the plates on the table. For there was a wee candle in a tiny candlestick beside the plate of each guest. These the guests could have to take home.

Some of the candles were yellow like dull gold. Some were blue. Perhaps Ruth's mother had chosen these two colors because Ruth liked them best.

The birthday cake was yellow with blue frosting. There were nine blue candles on the cake one for each of Ruth's nine years.

All these blue and gold-colored candles were made of the same kind of wax. The name of this wax is paraffin. Paraffin candles may be made in candle molds. Candle molds are metal tubes.

A wick is fastened through the center of each tube. Then the tube is filled with melted paraffin. As the paraffin cools it becomes a hard wax candle inside the mold. After the candle is taken out of the mold it is ready to use.

Old-fashioned candle mold and candlestick

Paraffin wax is white. But it can be colored with different dyes. So paraffin candles may have many different colors.

People melted other kinds of wax to pour into candle molds before they knew how to make paraffin candles.

They melted tallow and made tallow candles in molds, too. Tallow is a kind of fat.

Some candles are not made in molds. They are made by dipping the wicks into the melted wax or fat.

The wicks are cut the right length and tied to a stick. The stick is held over the melted wax or fat and the wicks are dipped into it. Then the wicks are lifted and the wax or fat cools. They must be dipped many times before the candles are thick enough to use. Such candles are called dips.

Candles made in molds are shaped by the molds. Dips are narrow at the top and thick at the bottom.

Making dips

After Ruth's pleasant birthday party was over, she read a story that was in a new book. She read the story by candlelight. She thought that was fun to do. At last it was time for her to say "Good night!" She thanked her mother for the party. "The lovely candles were a surprise," she said.

"Here is another surprise," said her mother. "Your grandmother sent you a birthday present."

Then Ruth's mother showed her a candlestick. It was the one Ruth's great-grandmother used when she was a little girl.

There was a dull green candle in the candlestick. It was the kind of candle that is called a bayberry dip.

A bayberry dip is made by dipping a wick into melted bayberry wax. Bayberry wax comes from a bush. The fruit of the bayberry bush is covered with wax. This wax is fragrant.

Ruth lighted the bayberry dip and took it to her bedroom. When she blew out the flame, the odor of the bayberry wax filled the air. She smelled this until she went to sleep.

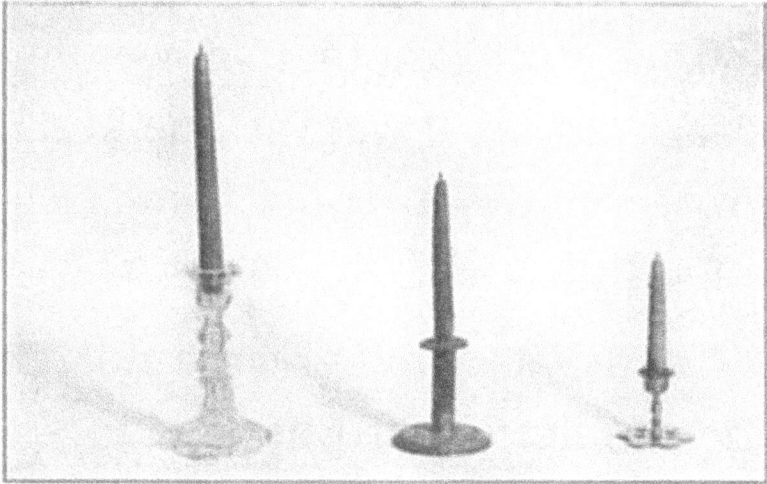

These candles are bayberry dips.

When Ruth's great-grandmother had been a little girl nine years old, she had never seen an electric light that could be turned on and off. She always went to bed by yellow candlelight. And sometimes her candle was a bayberry dip.

SCIENCE GAMES

1. Questions and Answers

On this page are four questions. One boy or girl may read a question. And another boy or girl may answer it.

1. What must be done to a cold stick before it can burn?

2. Once there were no matches to use. People did not know how to make matches then, but they knew how to start fires.

How could they start a fire with two pieces of wood?

3. How could they start a fire with hard stones called flints?

4. Why is it easier to start a fire with a match than with flints?

2. Fire and Air

In one chapter in this book you have read that things cannot burn without air.

Ask your teacher if she will help you with some experiments to see what happens to a fire when it does not have plenty of air.

An experiment is a test to find out a truth. On these pages are some tests to find out if it is true that a fire will go out if it does not have air.

1. Start a fire in a match head. Then squeeze the burning match head with a piece of cloth or some soft paper. What happens to the fire?

2. Start a fire with a match in the wick of a candle. Watch the flame.

3. Then cover the candle with a glass or a glass jar. The candle fire can have only what air there is in the glass or jar.

4. Watch the flame. Is there more smoke over the fire in the candlewick now?

5. Does the candle fire keep burning under the glass until the wax is all melted?

6. Twist a bit of paper and put it into a tin pan. Start a fire with a match. Press a piece of cardboard down on the fire. What happens to the fire? Why?

NEVER START A FIRE unless some grown person is with you and permits it!

SOME ANIMALS CALLED MAMMALS

1. Cows and Some of Their Relatives

Some animals have four legs or else two legs and two arms. They have warm red blood inside their bodies and some hair outside. Such animals are called mammals.

Mammals eat many different kinds of food when they are grown. But all mammals must have milk for food while they are babies.

A mammal mother has milk glands in her body where the milk is made. These milk glands have openings in them. A baby mammal can put its mouth about an opening and suck out milk.

That is the way a baby cow gets its first milk to drink. A baby cow, as you may know, is called a calf.

A calf takes milk from its mother.

A calf may be taught to drink milk out of a pail, too.

There were a cow and a calf at the farm where Ruth and Robert's grandfather lived. One day the children went to the farm to see the calf.

Grandfather said, "Robert, put on some old clothes and you may teach the calf to drink milk from a pail."

"Why do I need old clothes?" asked Robert.

All his grandfather said was, "You will see why you need them!"

Grandfather showed Robert how to teach the calf. First Robert dipped some milk in his hand and held it near the calf's mouth. The calf sucked the milk from Robert's fingers but it could not get much that way. It was very hungry and did not know how to get enough milk. So it pushed and bumped the pail. Some of the milk spilled over Robert's old clothes.

Grandfather and Ruth and Robert all laughed. The calf was very funny when it was pushing and bumping.

Robert held his handful of milk lower and lower in the pail. So the calf put its head down farther and farther to get it. Then Robert held his hand under the milk and the calf put its mouth against his hand and found the milk in the pail. The hungry baby was learning to drink.

A cow makes a great deal of milk in her glands. She has more than a calf needs. Men draw the milk out into pails. They take care of it and cool it and sell it.

People use milk to drink and to put into many foods they cook.

It is good for grown persons. But children need it even more. They should have good milk every day to help keep them well and strong.

People take goat's milk to use.

In many places people use only cow's milk. But in some places they take milk from goats and use that. Goat's milk is just as good for people's health as cow's milk.

In the far North it is too cold for cows or goats. It would be too hard to give them proper food and care. But reindeer can live there. So people in such places keep reindeer instead of cows or goats.

Reindeer eat grasses and sedges in summer. They like leaves of bushes. too. They are happy when people give them salt. In winter they dig through thick snow to get food. Under the snow, they find a kind of plant that is called reindeer moss.

All kinds of mammal mothers have milk for their own babies. But very few kinds have milk that people care to take and use for themselves.

Deer and goats are related to

The woman is milking a reindeer.

cows. They have feet with hoofs. They have horns on their heads. They have no front teeth in their upper jaws. Goats are more closely related to cows than deer are. Cows and goats have hollow horns.

2. Wolves and Foxes and Dogs

Robert and Ruth had never seen any wolves running together over snowy fields in winter. They had never seen even one lone wild wolf looking down from a cold hilltop. They had never heard a wolf howl.

But they had seen pictures of wolves. They had seen some stuffed wolves in a museum. And they had seen live wolves in a zoo.

Once these cousins had visited a fox farm. This was a place where a great many foxes were kept. They had small dark cages in which they could hide, and yards where they could run. A man gave them food when they were hungry.

Robert said, "I think wolves look very much like some kinds of dogs."

"The lone wolf"

"I think foxes look a little like some dogs, too," said Ruth.

There is a good reason why wolves and foxes should look much like dogs. They are related to dogs, and their bodies are alike in many ways.

124

Their feet and claws have about the same shape and their teeth are of the same sort. They like some of the same kinds of food and they have much the same way of eating it.

A small dog from Mexico

Chi was the smallest dog that Robert ever saw. He was not so large as a big cat. At first Robert thought Chi was a puppy. But he was really several years old and as large as he would ever grow. Chi had so little hair that his skin seemed almost bare.

You would not expect dogs like Chi to live in the far North, where the winters are long and cold. They could not keep comfortable in places like that. Most of them live in Mexico, which is a warm country.

Eskimo dogs like cold weather. Their fur is heavy and warm. They roll and dig and play in the snow.

Such dogs work as well as play. People who live in the snowy North teach Eskimo dogs to draw sleds with heavy loads on them. So when men need to take journeys across the snow they can put food and other things they need on their sleds. Then the dogs pull the sleds and help their masters that way.

Dogs love to do anything they can to please their friends. They have ways of making people understand them. They can call people by barking when they see something strange.

Mike was the name of an Airedale dog. One night when Mike was looking out a window, he began to bark. His master heard him and knew that the dog was trying to tell him to come to see what was happening.

So he looked out the window, too. He saw a fire at the edge of a field. Some dry grass was burning there, Then, of course, he ran to the field and put out the fire.

Mike's master thanked his dog. He said: "Mike, you are a good dog. You saw the fire and barked to tell me to come."

An Airedale dog like Mike

He put his hand gently on the dog's head while he praised him. Mike looked up and wagged his tail.

One day Miss Lee talked about dogs with the children in her room. She asked them which kinds of dogs they would have for pets if they could have their choice.

Some of the boys and girls chose little dogs and some chose big dogs. Some said they liked to see dogs with thick curly hair. Others liked those with smooth coats best.

They talked about how they could take care of their dogs and keep them well and happy.

Ruth said: "I think I'd rather have a Scottish terrier. I should call him Scottie or Mac if I had one. We could run and race and have jolly times together."

3. Horses and One of Their Relatives

Probably every child who reads this book has seen automobiles. Probably, too, you have all ridden in them. But perhaps some of you never rode in anything a horse pulled.

Yet not many years ago every one could see horses pulling carriages and busses and some kinds of cars, with people riding in them.

People no older than your grandfather and grandmother can remember when they rode in street cars that horses pulled along the tracks. In such a car there was no motor. So of course there was no motorman. Instead there was a driver with reins in his hands.

In those days horses pulled heavy wagons and light carriages along city streets and country roads. Farmers had many machines that horses could pull for them.

Horses are not needed in so many ways as they were once. We have better kinds of things to ride in, now, that horses do not pull. And there are bigger and stronger kinds of farm machines that are run with engines instead of horses.

But people still need these good animals for some kinds of work. And there are more of them in country places than in cities.

Long ago, the fastest way that a man had for getting from one place

Riding on a pony

to another was to ride on the back of a running horse. Many people still ride horseback. Some do so while they are busy with certain kinds of work. Others ride for pleasure.

One reason why Ruth and Robert liked to go to their grandfather's farm was that there were horses there. They loved these horses. They patted them and gave them lumps of sugar. The horses let them ride on their backs.

There was a pony on the farm, too. A pony is a very small kind of horse. Ruth and Robert took turns riding on the pony. He was gentle and never ran away. The children helped their grandfather take care of him.

Horses eat the same kinds of food that cows do. They like green grass and dry hay. They like different kinds of seeds that are called grain. They eat the same things but their mouths are not alike.

A horse has front teeth in its

upper jaw as well as in its lower jaw. It is different from a goat or a cow or a deer in other ways, too.

A horse's hoof is in one large part. It is not divided into smaller parts.

Zebras are related to horses.

When Robert and Ruth went to the zoo they saw an animal shaped much like a horse. It had stripes on its body. It was a zebra.

SCIENCE GAMES

1. Telling Fact Stories

A fact story is a true story. If you tell about the real shape and size of an animal, you tell facts about it. If you tell what an animal really does, you tell facts, too.

1. Did you ever watch a dog? If so, tell a fact story about the dog. Tell what sort of hair the dog had. Tell what you saw the dog do.

2. Did you ever see a cow or a calf? If so, tell a fact story about it. Tell how it looked and what it did.

3. If you ever saw a horse, a pony, or a zebra, tell a fact story about it.

2. Name These Pictures

1. You have read about dogs that live in the far North. Tell their name.

2. This animal is related to wolves and dogs. Can you tell its name?

3. Suppose You Were Blindfolded

Suppose some one were to tie a cloth over your eyes so that you could not see! Of course you could feel and hear and smell.

1. If some one put a puppy and a kitten in your lap, could you tell which was the puppy, even if you could not see? If you felt their feet, what difference would you find? What sounds would a kitten make that a puppy would not?

2. If some one led you to a colt (a young horse) and a calf, could you tell which one was the calf, even if you could not see? If you felt their teeth and their feet, what differences would you find in them?

AIR

1. Wind

"When I was very young," said Robert, "I thought a place was empty if it had nothing in it except air."

"I thought so, too," said Ruth, "when I was too young to know better! That was last year, I think."

The wind lifted and pushed the kites.

Ruth and Robert were flying their kites the day they talked about air.

"Wind is very strong," said Robert, as his kite pulled hard on its string. "And wind is nothing but moving air," said Ruth. "So air must be something, after all, or it could not move so fast and be so strong."

Very likely you, too, have thought about some of the things air can do when it moves.

You may have watched some clouds float slowly when there was a gentle breeze. You may have seen other clouds when they were carried swiftly by a very strong wind. And perhaps you have heard what a tornado can do.

Breeze and wind and tornado are just three different names for air when it is moving.

Many clouds form near oceans and large lakes. The wind carries some of these clouds to places a long way from large bodies of water.

The wind carries the clouds.

If the wind did not move the clouds, there would be too much rain near lakes and oceans. And there would be more places with almost no rain at all.

People find many uses for wind. If you watch a sailboat go or the wheel of a windmill turn, you will see two uses for moving air.

In some places it is easy for quiet air to become bad. If many people in a room breathe the same air, it is soon not fit to breathe any longer. There is not enough good gas in it.

Such air has a bad odor and it is harmful to breathe. The good gas that was in the air has been used.

So we need good ventilation in the rooms we use. A room has good ventilation when there are places for the bad air to go out and for good air to come in. There can be good ventilation only when air is in motion.

One way to change the air in a room is to open a window. Is that the way the air is kept good in your schoolroom? Or is there another way for keeping fresh air moving into your room and bad air moving out?

Wild animals have uses for moving air. The wind carries different scents as it moves. Some animals sniff the air to see how it smells. If they smell good food, they can go toward the wind to find it. If they smell the odor of some enemy, they can run the other way or hide by keeping very still.

Plants have uses for wind, too. Many plants travel by air when they move from one place to another. Of course, plants cannot do this when they are fastened to the ground by their roots. They can go on journeys only while they are seeds.

Miss Lee, Robert and Ruth's teacher, asked the children in her room how many different kinds of plants they could find with seeds that are carried by winds.

How many do you think they found? Perhaps if you hunt for different seeds that go sailing with the breezes, you will find some of the same kinds they did. Perhaps you will find some different kinds, too.

2. One Kind of Gas

Air does not need to be wind or even a breeze to be useful.

In another chapter in this book you read that a fire needs air when it burns. If you cover a fire with ashes or blankets or anything else that keeps the air away, you smother the fire.

There are different gases mixed in air. One of these is the gas that fire must have to keep it burning. The name of this gas is oxygen.

You must have this same gas to keep you alive. You draw air into your body through your nose. The air goes into your lungs. There the oxygen is taken up by the blood. The blood carries the oxygen for your body.

All animals must have this kind of gas. They get it from air, too. Of course many kinds of animals do not have noses and lungs. But they have other good ways of getting air.

You have only two holes in your nose to take air through. You have one other hole in your mouth.

Insects have more breathing holes in their bodies than you have in yours. Some of them have as many as twenty holes for breathing.

Each of these holes is the opening of a little breathing tube. The breathing tubes have branches that go to all parts of an insect's body.

Many insects can breathe in places where you would not have air enough.

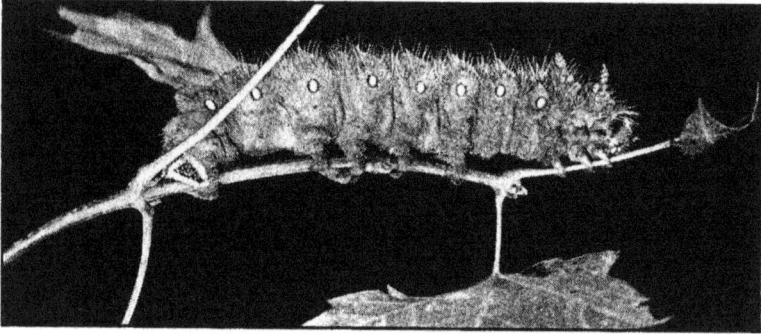

A caterpillar breathes through holes in its sides.

Some insects can breathe in the ground. Certain kinds can breathe inside galls on goldenrods or other plants. You would smother in such places.

You would smother, too, if your head stayed under water. But fishes can use the air that is mixed with water.

Animals living in different kinds of places must get oxygen from air in different ways. Each kind of animal has the sort of body that can breathe in the way that is best for it.

All plants must have the gas called oxygen. They cannot live without it.

Plants that have green leaves take in oxygen through their leaves. They take in this gas through their roots, too. There is air mixed with the soil that the roots can get.

Plants need oxygen as animals do. But plants need another gas, too. They take this other gas out of the air to use when they make sugar. So it helps them when they are making some of their food.

SCIENCE GAMES

1. A Toy Sailboat

Make a toy sailboat from pieces of wood. Use cloth for the sails. Put your boat in water where the wind can move it. If you cannot find a pond, a pan of water will do.

2. Questions about Air

1. Can you see pure air?

2. Can you smell it?

3. Can you taste it?

4. Can you feel air when it is quiet? Can you feel it when it is moving?

5. Can you hear air when it is not moving? Can you hear wind?

6. How can you tell that air is something real instead of just nothing at all?

7. Do you know what a weather vane is? If you do not know, ask some one to tell you how weather vanes are made and how they are moved by the wind. Ask some one to show you a weather vane.

3. Guess the Name

I stir the leaves upon the tree.
I'm mixed with water in the sea.

I carry clouds and scatter seeds.
Oh, every day I do good deeds!

No fire can burn unless I'm there.
I'm needed nearly everywhere.

For all the animals there are
And all the plants, both near and far,

Use a good gas I have to give.
And so I help them all to live.

Now think a while and then tell me
What you have guessed my name
      to be.

SOME INSECTS

1. Dragon Flies

There are many stories about fierce animals called dragons. Dragon stories are not fact stories because there never were any real dragons. But people liked to imagine queer terrible animals and they made pictures of them and told stories about them.

Certain insects have great glistening eyes and strong jaws. Their tails are shaped much like darning needles and look as if they might have big stings in them.

Some people thought "dragon fly" was a good name for such insects.

Other people thought that "darning needle" was a good name, too, and they made up some stories to go with that name. They said that these insects could sew up the ears or lips of bad children. But, as of course you know, that is only nonsense.

A dragon fly cannot harm anyone.

The end of a dragon fly's tail is not sharp. It has no sting at all.

Dragon flies have no wings while they are young. They live in ponds and rivers, then. They swim about and hunt for little water insects.

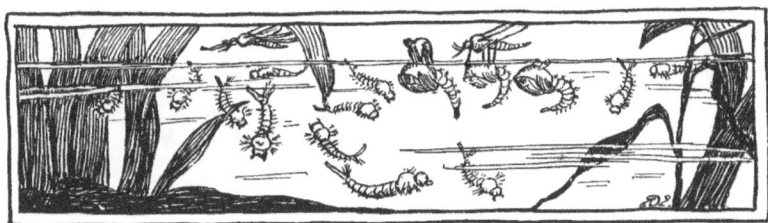

Wrigglers are young mosquitoes.

They like wrigglers to eat. Wrigglers are young mosquitoes. They live in the water until they are old enough to have wings and fly in the air.

Some kinds of dragon flies live in the water until they are about three years old. They can eat many wrigglers.

There would be more mosquitoes in the world to trouble us if there were no hungry dragon flies to eat them.

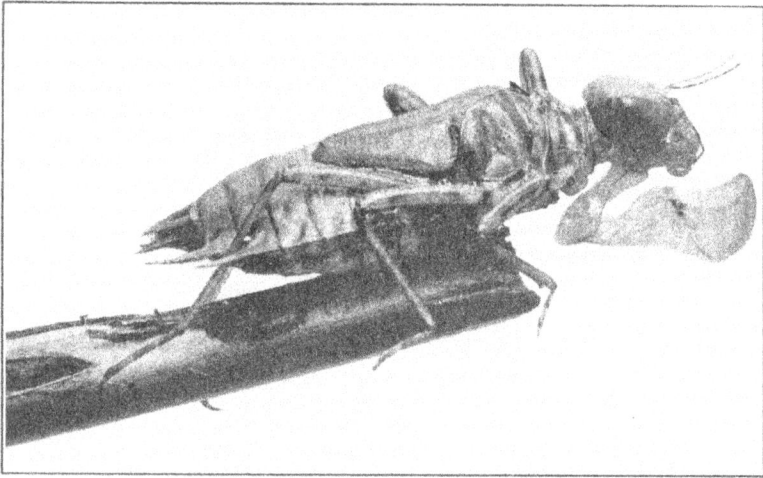

Young dragon fly waiting for its wings

When a dragon fly is old enough to have wings, it walks out of the water. It clings to a stem and waits. It does not need its swimming clothes any more. The time has come for it to have four beautiful wings.

After it has waited a little while, its swimming suit tears at the middle of the back. Then the grown dragon fly creeps out through the torn place.

At first its wings are soft and floppy but they soon become strong.

If you hunt near streams and ponds, you may find some of the empty suits that once covered young dragon flies.

You may see, also, some grown dragon flies hunting in the air for grown mosquitoes.

Now that you have read a chapter about dragon flies, you will see why some people call them mosquito hawks. And perhaps you will think that mosquito hawk is a very good name, too.

2. May Beetles

May beetles have thick brown bodies almost an inch long. In the daytime they fold their wings under their glossy brown wing covers and rest. But at night they lift their wing covers and spread their wings and fly about.

They like to fly by moonlight. They are hungry, then, and go to trees to eat leaves. They like plum and cherry and willow and some other kinds of leaves.

Their jaws make little clicking noises when they eat. Perhaps you will hear these queer sounds if you stand under a tree some night in May or June.

May beetles at night

There is another sound these beetles make. They hum with their wings when they fly. This is a sound that people often listen to in the evening. Poets like to hear it and write about it.

One poet wrote about an evening at sunset when
"All the air a solemn stillness holds
Save where the beetle wheels his
    droning flight."
Another poet once told about the
"beetle with his drowsy hum."
And still another poet said,
"O'er garden blooms,
On tides of musk,
The beetle booms adown the glooms
And bumps along the dusk."

Insects that fly by moonlight often make mistakes. They cannot tell the light of the moon from other lights. So sometimes these beetles fly to lighted windows and thump against the glass.

Or, if the windows are open, the beetles come into the room. Then they bump their heads against the wall and tumble to the floor. If they fall on their backs, they have a funny time turning over.

A May beetle is called a white grub while it is a larva or young insect. The white grub lives in the ground and eats the roots of grass and other plants.

It has a brown head and a fat

wrinkled white body. Its body is curved, so that the grub lies on its back or on one side while it eats.

When the grub is about three years old, it is as thick as a man's little finger. It is old enough then to turn into a pupa. So it makes a little cell in the ground and goes to sleep while its body changes its shape and its wings grow. Then, in May or June, it comes out of the ground and flies away to find juicy green leaves to eat.

Sometimes there are so many of these beetles that they harm trees by eating too many of their leaves. So it is a good thing for trees that nighthawks and owls and some

Moles and skunks hunt for white grubs.

other birds like May beetles to eat. These hungry birds help the trees by catching the beetles.

Often there are so many white grubs in the ground that they kill much of the grass in a field, or nearly all the strawberry plants in a garden.

So it is a good thing for plants that moles and skunks like to eat white grubs. Moles find these fat young insects when they are digging their holes underground. Skunks go into the fields at night or very early in the morning and roll back the sod with their paws and find the grubs. These hungry animals help plants by catching the white grubs.

3. Ruth Caught a Bumblebee

The apple tree in the corner of the yard was in blossom. The pink and white flowers were lovely. They were fragrant, too.

Ruth came into the yard. She stood in the sunshine and looked at the tree. She could smell the flowers. She wished she had one twig for her vase.

She stood on tiptoe but could not quite reach the lowest branch. So she jumped and caught the flowers in her hand. She caught something else, too. She caught a bumblebee!

The bumblebee was frightened but she could take care of herself. She thrust her sharp sting swiftly into

A bumblebee in an apple blossom

Ruth's hand. Then Ruth let go and the bee flew away.

Ruth gave a quick cry of surprise and pain. She looked at her hand. The place the bumblebee had pricked began to swell. It ached and throbbed.

There was a drug store on the next street where Ruth sometimes went. She went there now as fast as she could run. She showed her swollen hand to the druggist.

"Is a bumblebee sting very big?" she asked.

"No," said the druggist, "not nearly so large as the needle with which you often prick your finger."

"Then why does a sting hurt more than a needle?" asked Ruth.

The druggist told Ruth about bee stings.

A bumblebee has a little sac of acid inside her body near the sting. When the bee pushes her sting into anything, some of the acid pours out of the sac.

It is this acid that hurts and causes the swelling as soon as it gets into a wound.

Ruth knew about two kinds of acids. They were what made lemons and vinegar taste sour. She knew, too, that these acids hurt when they touched a cut or a scratch on her hand.

"Is the bee's acid like the acid of lemon or vinegar?" she asked.

"No," said the druggist. "The bee's acid is a different kind. It is called formic acid."

Bumblebees do not have all the formic acid. Many of their relatives have the same kind of acid in their bodies, too. Honeybees, yellow jackets and other hornets, wasps, and ants have formic acid to use when they need it.

They use this acid to defend themselves when they are frightened or in danger as the bumblebee was when she was caught in Ruth's hand. Of course Ruth did not intend to harm the bee. But the insect could not know what was going to happen.

Some kinds of ants defend

themselves by stinging, as many bees and wasps do. Other ants bite, instead, and use formic acid after they make wounds with their sharp little jaws.

Honeybees put formic acid into their honey. This keeps the honey fresh and good because then molds cannot grow on it and ruin it. The acid does not spoil the taste of the honey for the bees or for people either.

"Why doesn't the acid hurt my mouth when I eat honey?" asked Ruth.

"There is not enough for that," said the druggist. "It takes only a little formic acid to keep molds from growing."

After people learned about formic acid they found ways in which they could use it, too.

At first they did not know how to make it. So they took some from bees.

He handles honeybees carefully.

Some formic acid, too, they took from many ants that live in warm countries.

169

But after a while they learned how to make it for themselves in factories. Now they can have all they need.

When Ruth had first shown her hand to the druggist he had put a little cooking soda on the sore spot.

"The soda will destroy any acid there may be left on the outside of the wound," he said. "It will also make your hand feel cool and help it to heal more quickly."

"What will happen to the acid the bee put inside my hand where the soda can't reach it?" asked Ruth.

"Oh," the druggist told her, "your blood will carry it away as it flows through your body. Then the swollen place will get well."

SCIENCE GAMES

1. Lunches for Insects

Take some paper and make pictures of some insects eating their lunches. You may look at pictures in this book while you are making your own pictures if you wish.

1. Make a picture of a May beetle. Near the head of the beetle make a picture of something it likes to eat.

2. Make a picture of a white grub and show what it likes for food.

3. Make a picture of a butterfly near a flower that has nectar in it.

4. Make a picture of a caterpillar eating something that is good for it.

5. Make a picture of a dragon fly and show what it will eat.

2. Is It an Acid?

In the bumblebee chapter you read about an acid called formic acid. Some things are acid and some are not.

You can find out that some things are acid by tasting them. Many acids taste sour. Vinegar is a sour-tasting acid. Did you ever pull up a rhubarb stalk in the spring and taste it? There is a sour-tasting acid in the juice of the rhubarb plant.

But many kinds of acids are not in foods. Some kinds are painful poisons. And some acids do not taste sour. So, after all, tasting is not the best way to find out whether anything is acid.

A better way is to find out with litmus paper. Litmus paper is paper that has been colored with a blue dye called litmus. When a wet acid touches litmus it turns pink.

Ask your teacher if she will help you get some litmus paper and permit you to have some games with it.

1. Dip a narrow piece of litmus paper in pure water. Does the paper turn pink?

2. Put some lemon juice in the water. Test it with litmus paper. Does the paper turn pink? Is lemon juice acid?

3. Put some salt in water. Does the litmus paper turn pink in salt water?

WATER

1. Gas and Steam and Clouds

You have read about one kind of gas that is mixed in the air. There are many other kinds of gas in the world. Some of them are so common that you have them near you every day.

Sometimes water is a gas. Water is a gas when it is turned into steam. Steam is only very, very hot water.

You cannot pour steam into a glass. It will not run along in a stream like a little brook. It moves up into the air.

Water can be poured when it is not too hot or too cold. We say that water is a liquid when we can pour it.

You can change water from a liquid into a gas with heat. If you pour some water into a kettle and boil the water, you can easily change the liquid to steam that way.

A liquid is changed to steam by heat.

The steam does not stay in the kettle. It leaves the kettle and mixes with the air. If you boil the water long enough, it will all be gone after a while.

When the steam from the kettle moves in the air it becomes cool. Then it looks like a tiny cloud.

A cloud coming out of a steam engine

You can sometimes see bigger clouds coming out of a steam engine when a train goes by. The clouds from the kettle and the steam engine have little drops of water in them. The drops are so tiny and light that they can rise and float in the air.

The great clouds that you see far up in the sky have just such little drops of water in them, too.

Clouds have tiny drops of water in them.

Some of the water in the clouds far above us may come from kettles and steam engines and other places where people have made water so hot that it rises into the air.

But most of the water in the clouds does not come from places that people have made hot. Most of it gets up in the air without help from people.

When air touches water, tiny drops of the water go into the air. These drops may be so small that we do not see them.

The air touches wet clothes that some one has hung on a line. The water leaves the clothes and moves into the air. Then the clothes are dry.

But, of course, there is not enough water in wet clothes to make many of our great clouds.

The air moves across much water

in lakes and oceans. Part of the big clouds is made of water which rises from lakes and oceans.

Another place where air finds water is in the leaves of plants. All green leaves have water in them. The many, many leaves on thick forest trees have a great deal of water. So part of the clouds is made of water that rises from forests.

When water goes into the air from a boiling kettle, we may call it steam. We cannot see the steam that is nearest the spout. It soon cools to a little cloud of vapor that we can see.

Water that rises from oceans and forests may also be called vapor. Often it is called fog or mist.

White fog between the buildings and the hill

2. Liquid Water

You can change liquid water to gas by heating it. And you can change gas water to liquid by cooling it.

If you put an ice-cold glass in a warm room some hot summer day, little drops of water may settle on the outside of the glass. This is because the cold glass cools the air that is near it. And then the water that you cannot see in the air changes to drops that you can see.

When these drops are small enough they stay on the glass. But if they get large and heavy enough, they roll down the sides of the glass.

On summer nights, plants out-doors are cooler than they are on sunny days. The air near them becomes cooler, too.

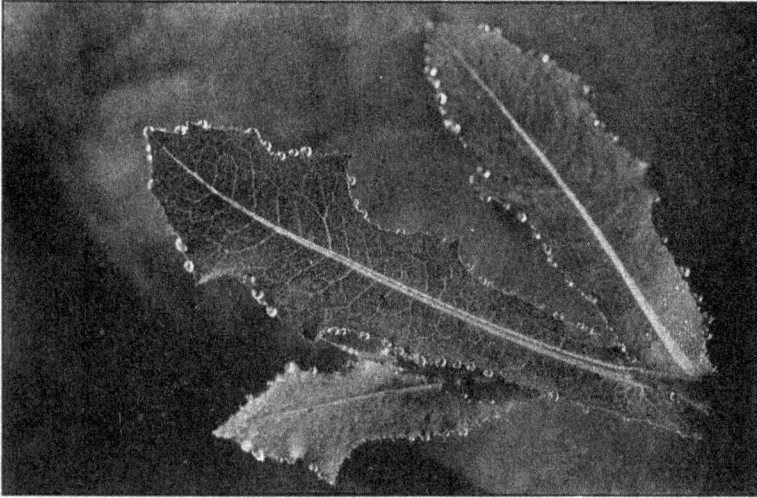

Leaves with dewdrops

So, very often, the water in this air settles on the leaves of the plants much as water settles on a cold glass in a warm moist room. Such drops of water on plants are called dew.

Clouds often become cool, too.

The air far above the earth is colder than the air that is near us. Some clouds are a mile or more above the earth. Air is cold, high overhead, even in summer weather.

Sometimes cool tiny drops of water in the clouds touch one another and run together to make bigger drops. They may become as large as raindrops. Then they are too heavy to stay up in the air. They fall as rain.

Some rain falls on the ground and soaks into the soil. Some runs into little brooks that pour into rivers and lakes. And at last the biggest rivers pour into the sea.

Then some of the water from the moist soil and from the sea and other wet places goes up into the air as gas, just as it did before.

All this happens over and over again, day after day. Water is going up as light gas all the time. Then it comes down again when it becomes too heavy to stay in the air.

Every plant must have some water. Plants with green leaves above ground and with roots underground take most of their water from the soil. Their roots have a way of drinking it. Then it is carried up the stem to other parts. The juices and other moist parts of plants are mostly water.

So rain is a very good thing for plants. In many places there is no other way for them to get enough water to keep them alive.

We need many kinds of plants for food. What should we do if there were not enough rain so that potatoes and spinach and carrots and cabbage and other good vegetables could grow?

Could we get along without corn and oats and wheat and all the other seeds we need for our own food or to give to cows and horses and other animals?

Animals need water to keep them alive just as much as plants do. Blood and other moist parts of the bodies of animals are mostly water.

Some kinds of animals get all the water they need by living in wet places and eating wet food. But many kinds do not get their liquid that way. Some get their water by drinking it when they are thirsty.

We need to drink water.

So you can see why Robert said, one day when he was thirsty, "I'm glad that water can go up into the air as gas and then come down again as such a good liquid to drink!"

3. Solid Water

Water is solid when it is so cold that it is frozen. Frozen water has different names. Some of them are ice and hail and snow and frost.

Ice is not quite so heavy as liquid water. That is the reason that ice stays at the top of a lake or a river.

If ice were heavier than water and sank, people could not skate on it. That would take some of the good times away from winter. Many boys and girls could not have so much fun in cold weather.

The fishes and other water animals could not have a good time, either. If the ice sank or the water froze around them, they could not live.

But the ice makes a cover over a river or lake. The fishes can swim in the water under the ice.

Sometimes raindrops freeze when they are high in the air. Then they come falling down to the ground and we say we have a hailstorm. This can happen on a summer day if the air near the clouds is cold enough.

Hail strikes much harder than rain does. It sometimes harms plants and other things by breaking them.

In winter we do not often have hail. In the North where winters are cold we have snow instead. That is because the water in the air freezes before it gets together in big raindrops.

Snowflakes have beautiful shapes.

It freezes in tiny thin pieces that we call snowflakes.

Snowflakes have many beautiful shapes. You can see that they are lovely with just your eyes. You can see even better if you have a reading glass to look through, because they seem larger through such a glass.

Snow on the ground is good for plants that live in the North. It is like a thick blanket to keep their roots from being too cold.

In the spring the snow melts and some of the water soaks into the ground. Then the plants can drink it with their roots.

Some of it runs away into little

You can often find frost on plants.

streams. The streams pour into rivers. Some of the snow water pours into lakes and last of all it reaches the sea.

You cannot find dew on cold winter mornings. But you can often find frost instead. You can find it on the stems of trees and bushes and in many other places.

One good place to look is on a window glass. Sometimes the frost makes wonderful pictures there.

Ruth and Robert both liked frost pictures. They had many good times looking at them.

Sometimes they thought of stories to go with the white pictures on the window glass.

SCIENCE GAMES

1. Vapor

Ask some one at home if you may play these four games with water.

1. Pour a cup of water into a pan. Place the pan on a hot stove. See how many minutes it takes all the water to change to vapor and leave the pan.

2. Pour a cup of water into the same pan. Put the pan on a shelf or table or some other cool place. Look at it once in a while to see about how many hours or days it takes all the water to leave the pan.

3. Take two handkerchiefs or two towels that are alike. Put them

into water and then wring them so that they do not drip. Hang one out straight on a line so that the air touches both sides of it. Fold the other one so that it is thick before you fasten it on the line.

Does the folded handkerchief or towel dry more quickly than the one that is spread out? Or does it take the folded one longer to dry?

Can you tell why one dries more quickly than the other?

4. Pour a cup of water on a board or a sidewalk in a sunny place.

Pour a cup of water on a board or a sidewalk in a shady place.

Does the water change to vapor faster in the sun or in the shade?

2. A Puzzle

Read all the lines on this page. Then think of one word that will be the right name for the gas and the liquid and the solid.

I may be gas. I rise from seas.
I go away with every breeze.
You call me vapor when you please.

I may be liquid, as in dew
Or drops of rain. And it is true
You bathe in me and drink me, too.

I may be solid, as in snow
Or ice. As hail, I patter so
You hear me on the roof, I know.

Solid or liquid or a gas — all three
Yet one name is enough for me!

Clouds, snow, mountain, and lake

SOME ANIMALS WITH FEATHERS

1. Goslings and Chickens

Some fluffy goslings lived on a farm. They were the young of Mother Goose and Father Gander. They did not stay in the nest after they were hatched. They were ready to go for a walk with their father and mother soon after they were out of the eggshells and their downy feathers were dry.

The old geese often walked in grassy places, for they liked tender grass to eat as well as cows and sheep do. So the goslings had pleasant walks in the meadow. They had good times catching insects to eat.

197

Goose, gander, and goslings

Both the parent birds helped take care of the goslings. When Father Gander saw a dog or a cat come near, he would put his head and neck down low and say, "Hiss-s-s!" He would wiggle his long neck like a snake. Then he would run after the animal and chase it away. If it didn't go fast enough, he would nip it with his bill and whip it with his wings.

But when Father Gander felt very happy he had something else to say. He would stand straight and hold his head high and flap his big wings and call, "Honk! Honk!"

The little goslings and the old geese all had flat feet like paddles and their bodies were somewhat boat-shaped. You could tell by looking at them that they did not spend all their time walking in meadows. They liked to swim, too. Indeed, they enjoyed the water so much that they often stayed there nearly all day.

Wild geese swimming in a pond

They caught insects and other little animals in the water and found some in the mud. They ate some of the tender water plants, too.

The downy young chickens at the farm were nearly as fluffy as the goslings. But their feet did not have the same shape and they could not swim. Their bills were different, too.

Mother hen and chickens

They had feet for scratching and bills for pecking, like those of Mother Hen and Father Rooster.

At first they could not scratch hard or deep. Their mother found food for them. She scratched for worms and grubs and underground caterpillars. When she found one of them she held it in her bill and called, "Cluck, cluck!" The chickens answered her by saying, "Peep, peep," and they ran to get their food.

Father Rooster did not stay with the chickens. He woke very early every morning and crowed. He called before the sun was in sight. He shouted for joy as soon as the sky began to be light in the east. His crowing was his morning song.

Ruth and Robert liked to watch the goslings and chickens at the farm.

The young farm birds learned to take food from their hands.

Father Rooster was glad every morning.

Robert said, "It is easy to tame farm birds. Perhaps we can help take care of some wild birds so they will like us, too."

2. Helping Wild Birds

Two of the birds that Robert and Ruth helped were tree swallows.

Robert made a box for their home. His grandfather showed him how to do it.

The floor of the box was five inches on each side. It was a square floor. The sides of the box were six inches high between the floor and the roof. The birds needed an open door through which to go in and out. So Robert cut a hole that was one and one-half inches square.

The pair of tree swallows liked this box. While the mother bird hunted for soft bits of hay and other fibers for the nest, the father sat on a twig and sang a gentle twittering song. He watched the box. When some other birds came too near, the father swallow flew to the door hole and would not let them go in.

Father Swallow watched the nest box.

Ruth found soft white feathers. She tossed some of them into the air and the tree swallows flew and caught them.

After the swallows were used to flying near Ruth for the feathers, she held some in her hand. One of the birds came and took one from her fingers. The tree swallows liked white feathers best of all to line their nest.

An oriole likes short string to use.

The children helped a pair of orioles, too. They cut some string into pieces ten or twelve inches long.

That was a good length for the birds to use without getting tangled in it. The children put the cut string on some bushes and watched an oriole come for it.

One day in June, Robert was visiting the farm. He heard a bird making a queer sound. The bird seemed to be fussing and teasing. She was pulling at a long piece of string that had been tied around a branch. She wanted the string but could not get it. She scolded and teased in a low voice.

Robert watched the bird and saw what she was trying to do. He said "Don't be so worried and disappointed. I'll cut the string for you."

The waxwing used some string in her nest.

So Robert cut the string in short lengths, which he left on the branch. He hid behind some bushes and watched. In a little while the bird came back and took the string. This time she seemed happy.

Robert had a good chance to look at the bird. She had a crest of feathers on her head like a little pointed cap. Most of the feathers on her head were soft grayish brown. Most of the feathers of the wings and tail were gray. But the tip of the tail was yellow and some of the wing feathers had bright red spots at the tips. These red spots looked like hard shiny bits of sealing wax. That is the reason this kind of bird is called a waxwing. Its full name is cedar waxwing.

Robert watched to see where the waxwing flew with the string and he found that she was making her nest on a branch of a maple tree. The nest was made with strips of bark and old grass and other fibers besides the string.

Grandfather said: "Waxwings are beautiful birds. I like to see them. They are helpful, too. They eat many of the caterpillars that trouble apple and other orchard trees.

"These birds like to eat ripe cherries and I am glad to spare some for them. They earn them by taking care of the trees.

"But I think it would be a good way for you and Ruth to help birds if you will find out what small berries they like to eat. Then we can plant more of the trees and bushes that have their favorite berries. Perhaps they would not eat so many of the cherries then."

So whenever Ruth and Robert came to the farm they watched the birds to see what berries they liked.

And early the next spring their grandfather set out a long row of young bushes and trees for the birds.

Spring was a good time to do this on his land. There was some clay in the soil and the ground was wet for a long time in the spring.

So the roots of the bushes and trees had a good chance to grow before summer.

There were mulberry trees and chokecherry trees in the row. There were elderberry bushes and many other bushes that would have berries.

"I'll plant a row of the kind called high-bush cranberries," said Grandfather. "They have sour berries that stay on all winter. Some birds will come for those when the ground is covered with snow."

"And please plant a great many twin-flowered honeysuckle bushes," said Ruth. "We saw bluebirds and robins and thrushes and waxwings all eating honeysuckle berries."

SCIENCE GAMES

1. Which?

1. Does an oriole or a tree swallow build a nest in a bird box?

2. Does a gander or a rooster crow in the morning?

3. Does a goose or a hen take her young to swim?

4. Does a gosling or a chicken scratch with its feet?

5. Does an oriole or a cedar waxwing have a crest on its head?

6. Does a hen or a goose say, "Cluck!" to her young?

7. Does a gander or a rooster say, "Hiss-s-s!" when he is not pleased?

2. Look at the Picture

High-bush cranberries

High-bush cranberries are not real cranberries. Real cranberries grow on low plants. Look at the picture on this page and then tell a story about it.

In your story, tell why some people plant these bushes. Tell whether there is anything on these bushes in the winter. Tell why some birds like to visit them.

FINDING ROCKS

1. Chalk

One day Robert said to his teacher, "Miss Lee, I wish we could all go into the country and hunt for different kinds of rocks."

Miss Lee asked, "Wouldn't it be just as much fun to find rocks in the city?"

"Where could we hunt?" asked Ruth.

Ruth held a piece of chalk in her hand. She had been writing with it.

Miss Lee laughed. She had a pleasant way of laughing. The boys and girls liked to hear her. Then she said, "Ruth, you might begin to hunt by looking in your hand."

Ruth was surprised. "Is chalk a rock?" she asked.

Then Miss Lee told the boys and girls about chalk. She told them what it is and where it is found.

In some parts of the world there are great hills of chalk. Very often one side of such a hill is a steep bank or cliff.

Some kinds of birds like to make their nests in a chalk cliff. This white stuff is a soft kind of rock. Some birds can dig little caves in it with their bills. They put their nests in the caves.

Long, long ago these chalk hills were not on top of the ground where birds could fly to them. They were once at the bottom of the sea, where fishes swam over them.

There were other sea animals besides fishes there, too, of course. Many of them had shells. Some had shells with pretty twisted shapes, like snail shells. Some had shells in two halves with a hinge on one side, like oyster and clam shells. Some were large and some were little.

Some were so tiny that their shells were smaller than the heads of common pins. There were millions and millions of them. They lived most of the time near the top of the water.

When one of these tiny animals died, its shell dropped to the bottom of the sea.

A chalk cliff

There were so many shells dropping that they went down through the water somewhat like snowflakes falling through the air. They lay on the bottom of the sea in thick beds, as snow lies on the ground in piles.

Larger shells went to the bottom of the sea, too; but there were not so many of those. And so, year after year, the bottom of the ocean was covered deeper and deeper with shells. Those that were on top pressed down on those beneath. And after a while the shells were not loose any more. They were pressed together into white soft rock.

Many parts of the earth that are now dry ground were once covered by the sea. In some places the sea is lower and the land is higher than it once was. And that is the way with the high chalk hills.

Not all of the chalk is in hills on land. There is a great deal of it still at the bottom of the sea. Little shells still drop and drop and make new chalk.

At first people used to write with chalk just as it came from a cliff. But now a great deal of the chalk is ground to a fine powder and mixed with wax or soap or something else. Then it is pressed into pieces like thick pencils. Such chalky pencils are often called crayons. Some crayons are dyed different colors.

2. Clay and Slate

Robert had some clay. He liked to make it into different shapes.

One rainy Saturday he made some little toy animals with his clay. He liked his elephant best. So he took it to school Monday and showed it to Miss Lee.

"Do you know where clay comes from?" asked Miss Lee.

"I think it is a sticky kind of mud that men dig out of the ground," said Robert.

"So it is," said Miss Lee. "But the stuff such mud is made from was once part of hard rocks."

Rocks may be broken in different ways.

Sometimes mountains are covered with ice. The ice may be so thick that it is like a mountain of ice on top of a mountain of rock.

Sometimes ice from the mountains reaches the sea.

When such ice moves slowly down the side of a mountain it breaks off parts of the rock. The broken rocks are carried along by the moving ice.

They hit against other rocks and are broken still more. Some of the rocks may be crushed into small pieces like pebbles and sand.

Hard rocks may break and crumble.

Many rocks are cracked by frost and some are split by lightning.

Rocks may fall to pieces, too, because of what rain and air do to them. Perhaps you know that hard iron things change to brown powder when they are left in moist places where they rust. Rocks may crumble in much the same way.

Much of the fine stuff from rocks that were broken many, many years ago became soaked with water and changed in different ways into clay.

When certain kinds of clay are heated they become hard like rock.

Men make bricks with clay and bake them in outdoor ovens. They make some kinds of dishes of clay and heat them until they have become hard.

A kind of rock called slate has been made from clay. But men did not make it. Slate was made long ago without any help from men.

Slate rocks

In some places there were great beds of clay where the earth was pressed and rubbed together until it became hot.

This hot pressed clay became baked in the earth. When it became cool it was not sticky mud any longer. It was the rock which we call slate.

Although men had nothing to do with pressing or baking slate, they have many ways of using it. Perhaps you have seen a house with slate on the roof instead of wooden shingles.

There was a slate blackboard in Miss Lee's schoolroom. So the children did not need to go outdoors to find this kind of rock. It was close at hand.

3. Coal

All the boys and girls in Miss Lee's room tried to find different kinds of rocks. They could see many kinds, out of doors or at home or in stores, that they could not have to take to school. But other kinds they could bring to show to one another.

Some of the children brought pieces of coal. So Miss Lee told them about that kind of rock.

You have seen flowers with bright colors.

You know that oak and maple trees and other kinds, too, have thin broad leaves.

But there have not always been plants with bright flowers and trees with broad leaves on the earth. Once there were none. That, of course, was long, long ago.

In those days the plants were different from any we can see to-day. We do not even know how many of those plants looked. But we know some things about the shapes and sizes of some of them.

There were fern-like plants as big as giant trees growing, then.

Other plants that grew as large as tall trees had hollow stems with joints in them. There are small relatives of such plants growing now. We call them horsetails.

Small plants called club mosses grow in some places now.

We call them horsetails.

But once plants like club mosses grew to the size of great trees.

Those trees like ferns and horsetails and club mosses grew in forests. The forests were in wet swampy places. Some of them were near the sea.

When a tree in such a forest died, it fell and lay on the ground. After the trees had been growing and falling for a great many years, they became very deep on the ground. They made thick beds. In many places the ground sank and sea water covered it.

Then sand and mud from crumbling rocks were carried by the water of rivers to the sea. It settled over the beds of fallen plants.

More and more sand and mud came, so that it became heavier and heavier. It pushed down on the plants and crushed them. At last the fallen plants were pressed and changed until they were a hard black kind of rock. We call that hard black rock coal.

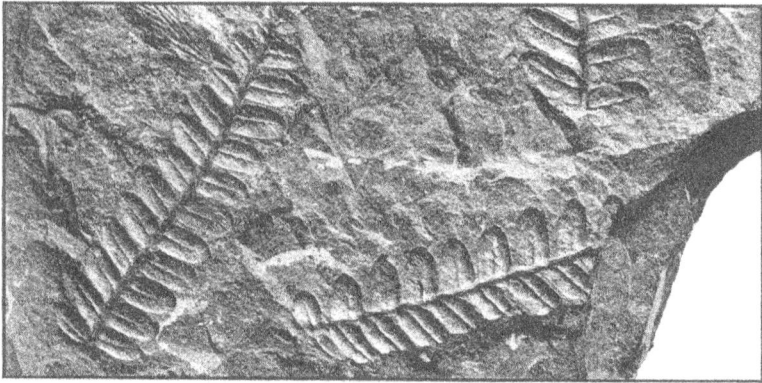

Fern fossils in coal

We know that there are hardened plants in coal. Some of their shapes still show before the coal is broken into small pieces. We call them fossils.

Most coal mines where men dig coal are not under the sea, now. That is because the sea does not cover all the parts of the earth it once did.

A coal mine

There are coal mines on dry ground now where there was once water, just as there are dry chalk cliffs, now, that used to be at the bottom of the sea.

4. Coral and Limestone and Marble

Ruth's mother had some red coral beads. She let Ruth wear them about her neck to school one day.

Miss Lee asked Ruth to show the coral beads to the other children. Then she told them about coral.

There are some little animals living in the sea that have corals for their skeletons. These animals are very little and their bodies are very soft.

There are holes in the coral. The little animals can pull their soft bodies into the holes and hide. Or they can push their feelers out into the water when they catch their food.

Great numbers of these little animals live near one another in colonies.

Some coral animals

235

They grow so close together that their coral is together in one piece like a big rock with many tiny holes in it.

The young coral animals put their new skeletons on top of old coral and, after a long time, there are so many of these all together that they make hills of coral rock in the sea.

There are different kinds of coral animals with different shapes and colors of coral. Some coral is red, some is pink, and some is nearly black. A common kind is white.

Coral animals are living in warm ocean water, now. They build their hills of coral rock year after year, in many places.

There were coral animals living in the sea thousands of years ago, building the same kind of hills.

Some of those old hills that were once covered with water now have their tops sticking out above the sea. So they are coral islands.

And some of the great beds and hills of coral are not in the sea at all any more. They are on dry land. But they do not look like coral, now. There are no little coral animals living in them. Sea shells and other things have been mixed with the coral and it is all changed to a kind of rock we call limestone.

There are some kinds of sea plants that were changed to limestone, too.

Limestone is a good kind of rock to use in building stone houses.

A limestone house

In some places the limestone has been changed slowly. Where the earth became very hot and the heated limestone was pressed together hard enough, another sort of rock was made. This rock is called marble.

Sometimes marble is cut into large blocks and polished until it is smooth and shiny. Such blocks are often used in making the walls of very grand and handsome buildings.

A marble monument

Marble can be cut in different shapes. Beautiful ornaments are made from it. This kind of rock is often used for statues, too.

SCIENCE GAMES

1. Hunting for Rocks

Try to find the same kinds of rocks about which you have read in chapters of this book. Try to find other kinds, too.

1. Have you and your school-mates any little balls which you call marbles? If you have, show them to one another.

Ask some one to tell you whether any of these little balls are made of real marble.

Ask if some of your marbles are made of clay and baked until they are hard.

Have you any agate marbles? Ask some one to tell you about agate.

2. If you live in the country, hunt near your home for as many kinds of stones as you can find.

3. If you live in a city, hunt in a park for different little stones, if you are permitted to do so.

4. Look in stores for different things that are made from any kind of rock.

5. Look in your own home for different things that are made from some kind of rock.

6. Find in your schoolhouse things made from rock, if you can.

7. Hunt for buildings with rocks in their walls.

8. Make a list of all the kinds of rocks you have found.

2. What Is It Called?

Here are the names of four kinds of rock. Copy the lines on this page and put each name in its right place.

coal   marble   chalk   slate

1. One kind of rock has tiny sea shells in it. It is a white rock called ****.

2. One kind of rock has parts of old plants in it. It is a black rock which we burn. It is called ****.

3. In some places clay was heated in the earth and pressed into a hard dark rock called ****.

4. Some limestone was heated and pressed in the earth. In this way it was changed to ****.

3. Rhymes about Rocks

Here are some rhymes about rocks. The last word is left out of each rhyme.

Copy the rhymes on paper and write a good word for each empty place.

Some day, perhaps, I'll take a walk
And see a great white cliff of ****.

I may look down in some deep hole
Where men are busy mining ****.

Slate is a kind of rock, they say,
Made long ago from heated ****.

Chalk now in dry high banks may be,
But once it was in the deep wet ****.

I saw some marble. How it shone!
And once 'twas only rough lime ****.

EARTH, SUN, MOON, AND STARS

1. Our Earth

The sun and moon and stars do not rest on any solid foundation. There is space on all sides of them.

There is space all around our earth, too. There is air that we can breathe near the earth. But the space farther away is without such air.

The earth is moving all the time in this space. It moves around the sun in a circular path. It travels faster than a thousand miles a minute. This is very, very fast but the journey is so long that it takes the earth twelve months to circle around the sun. It goes around the sun once every year.

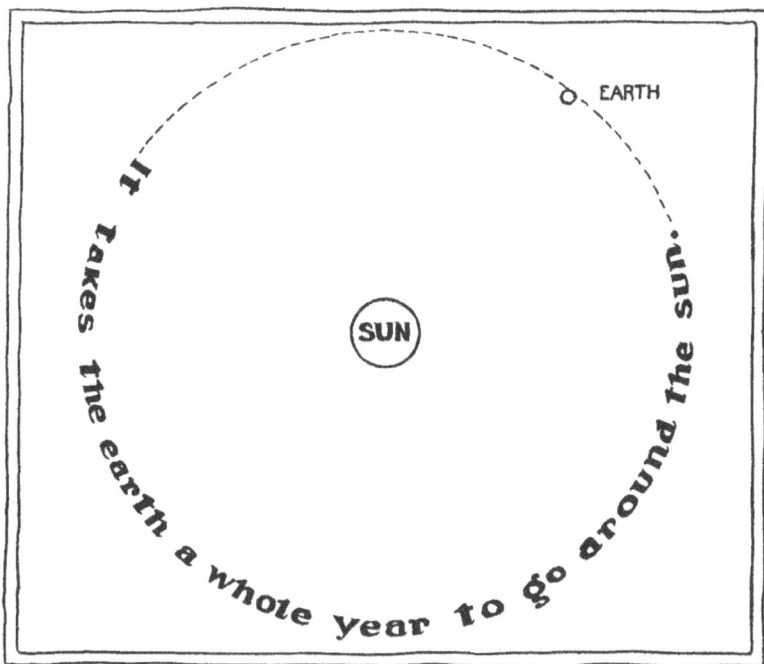

The earth is round. It spins or whirls as it goes. Its spinning motion is much like the motion of a whirling top. A top is so small that it can spin around once in a very short time.

But the earth is so large that it takes it twenty-four hours, or one whole day, to spin around once.

We say the sun is rising.

When the earth is turned so that we see the sun in the east, it is morning on our part of the earth. We say the sun is rising, but really the earth is turning toward the sun.

It is noon for us when the earth has turned so that we look high overhead to see the sun.

When the earth has turned so that we look toward the west to see the sun, it is our evening and we say the sun is setting.

After the earth has turned so that we cannot see the sun at all, it is night. People on the other side of the earth can see the sun then. It is daytime for them while it is night for us.

The earth is a planet. The word planet means a wanderer. There are other planets, besides the earth, that circle around our sun.

As you have read, it takes the earth three hundred sixty-five days, or twelve months, or one year, to take one journey around the sun.

Another planet, which is nearer the sun, moves around it in eighty-eight days.

Where did the earth come from? Some men who know most about suns and planets say that they think the earth was once a part of the sun. They say that the earth was whirled away from the sun.

When that happened the earth was as hot as the sun. It was so hot it was not solid. The whole earth was made of gases then.

After a time the hot gas earth began to be less hot. Some of the gases mixed together and made air. Some joined each other and made water. And some joined one another and made certain kinds of solid rocks.

No one knows how long all these changes took. But there came a time when the earth was cool enough so that plants and animals could live on it. There was air to breathe and water to drink. There were the ocean and solid ground.

There is no one who knows how long ago it was when plant life and animal life first began on our earth.

But now the earth is so cool that the animals and plants living here need the warmth from the sun for life.

2. Our Sun

You cannot look at the sun at noon on a bright day without hurting your eyes, unless you look through a darkened glass. But you can look at it very early in the morning or just before it disappears in the evening.

How large does the sun look to you? Does it look as if a foot ruler or a yardstick would be long enough to reach across it?

Of course the reason the sun does not look larger to our eyes is that it is so far away. The farther away a thing is, the smaller it looks to us.

The sun is over three hundred thousand times as large as the earth.

It is a gigantic glowing ball of thick heavy hot gases. Flames shoot out from the sun much faster than a bullet shoots out from a rifle.

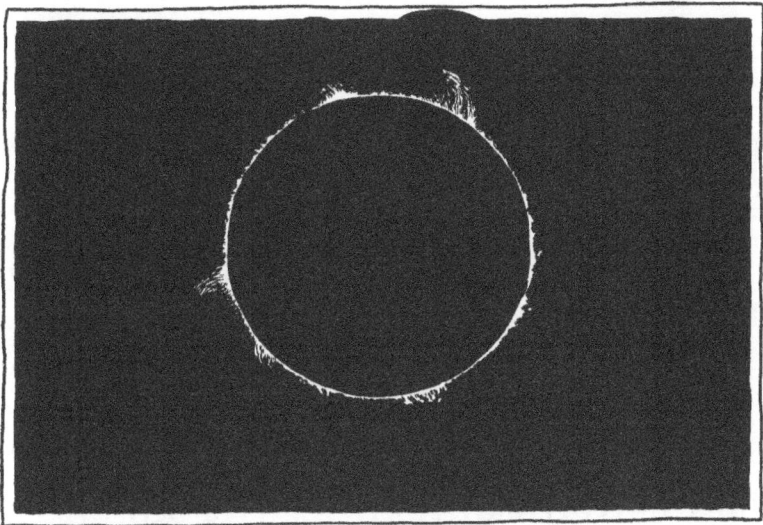

Flames shoot out from the sun.

These flames are many thousands of miles long.

If we try to think how hot the sun must be, we are glad that we are so far away. If we were too near, we could not live on the earth. But if the earth were too far away, we could not live here either. For then it would be too cold.

In another chapter in this book, you read that plants can make sugar in their green leaves while the sun shines on them. They cannot make sugar in the dark.

Other changes take place in plants in the sunshine. The sunshine causes changes to take place in the bodies of animals, too.

You can feel the heat from the sun on your skin when you stand in the sunshine on a summer day. Your skin becomes darker if you play much in the sunshine. You say you are tanned. It is very good indeed for you to have tanned skin.

Some sunshine is good for you.

However, if you stay too much in the sunshine when you are not used to it, your body may become blistered and sore. Sometimes people are made ill by lying too long on the seashore.

Not enough sunshine is bad for people, too. Babies who do not have enough sunshine are likely to have weak and crooked bones.

In this country people who work or play outdoors get all the sunshine they need, especially in summer time. The sunshine is not so bright in some countries where there is more moisture in the air than we have in the United States.

Children living in such places often have weak bones, unless they are given good care to make up for the lack of sunshine.

One way to give them good care is to let them have light rays from certain electric machines. The light from these machines has certain of the same kinds of good health rays that sunlight has.

Some doctors keep such electric machines in their offices. People sometimes have them in their homes.

Schools, in some places, have them, too. Children in such schools let the health rays shine on them for a very short time each day. That helps keep them well even in winter and in cloudy weather.

Some foods act on the bodies of animals in some of the same ways that health rays do. Cod liver oil is such a food. You may know people who take cod liver oil in winter. Perhaps you have taken some yourself.

Do you know what people mean when they say that you get the warmth of stored sunshine when you burn wood or coal? They mean that the trees which are cut for wood could not have grown if there had been no sunshine. The great ferns and trees and other ancient plants that became hardened into coal could not have grown, either, except for sunshine.

The more you learn about the sun and the warmth and light and health in sunshine, the gladder you may feel when you look toward the east in the morning or toward the west at the close of day. It may give you happiness to see the sun.

3. Our Moon

The moon is the nearest neighbor the earth has. It is much nearer than any planet or star or sun. But it is not very near.

If there were a road to the moon and we could travel there by automobile, the journey would take a long time. It would take us nearly half a year to reach the moon if the automobile went sixty miles an hour and we never stopped to rest.

What should we find if we could go to the moon? We should find great mountains with deep hollows in them. Some of the mountains are higher than the highest mountains on the earth.

People can see these moon mountains without leaving the earth. They look through telescopes to see them. Telescopes have glass in them. The glass is shaped to make things look nearer and larger.

Bird glasses or field glasses make things look a little larger and nearer but they are not so powerful as the telescopes.

People have named the moon mountains. They have given them the same name as some mountains on this earth. There are mountains called Alps on the earth and on the moon, too.

There are many photographs of the mountains and the valleys of the moon. They are taken with cameras that are attached to telescopes. Such a picture is shown on this page.

Circular places on the moon that have rock walls thousands of feet high

Men have maps of the moon, too. They look at the moon through telescopes and then draw pictures of what they are able to see. So people know how to find their way on the moon even though they can never go there.

The moon is round like a huge ball. It moves around the earth in a somewhat circular path.

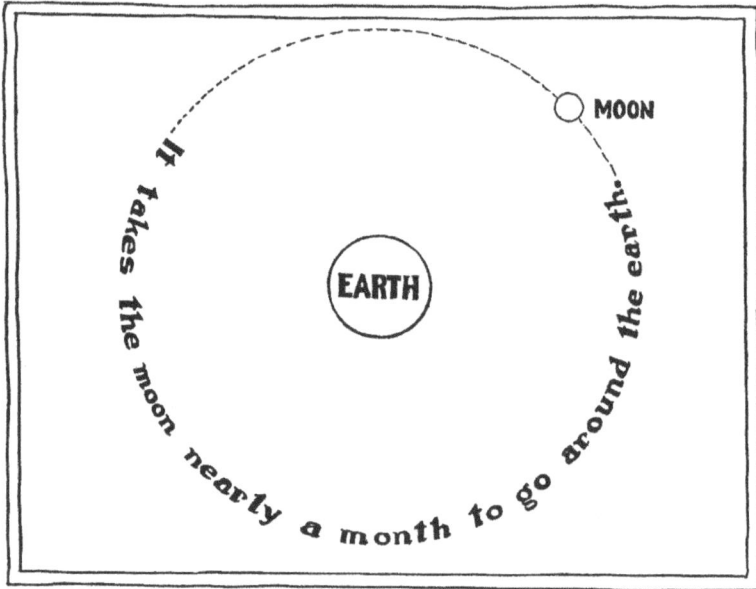

It takes the moon nearly a month to travel around the earth.

About once a month we say we have a new moon. And about once a month we say this moon is full.

Of course we do not really have a different moon once a month. Our moon is always the same one. The moon, itself, is just the same on the nights we call it "new" and on the nights we call it "full."

The sun shines on the moon as it does on the earth. The half of the moon that is toward the sun is light. The half that is turned away from the sun is dark.

The whole round light half of the moon is turned toward the earth as well as toward the sun when we say the moon is full.

At other times only part of the light half of the moon is turned toward the earth.

The crescent moon

At first, each month, we see what we call a crescent. That is when we can see only the curved edge of the light part. A few nights later, we can see about a quarter of the moon. Later still, we can see about half of it. Then, at last, it looks round to us. We gaze at it and say, "The moon is full to-night."

The night does not seem very dark when the moon is full and the air is clear. We can easily see our way to walk by moonlight. We can see certain colors by the light of the moon. Some trees in fall are pretty to look at when the moon shines on their colored leaves. Sometimes moonlight is so bright that we can even see by it to read the pages of a book.

But none of this light is really made by the moon itself. It is really light from the sun that shines on the moon. It is reflected by the moon.

If you put a lighted candle or other light in front of a mirror, you can get light from the mirror. But the mirror has no light of its own. It can only reflect the light that shines on it. Mirrors reflect light clearly.

A mirror can reflect light.

There are many other things that can reflect light, too. You can see light reflected by water and by shiny metals.

Our earth, itself, does not give light. But it can reflect the sunlight that shines on it. If we could visit the moon and look at the earth, the earth would seem bright like a moon. It would be reflecting sunlight.

So in the daytime we have direct light from the sun. And at night we have sunlight reflected by the moon.

Of what is the moon made? Some men who have studied the earth and the moon think that once the moon was part of the earth. They think that some of the earth became loose enough to be thrown way off into space while the earth was spinning very, very fast.

Some men think that the moon was thrown off while the earth was still a mass of hot gases. The moon was more like the sun then. Other men think that the moon did not whirl away from the earth until some later time, when the mass was cooler.

We have one day in our week named for the sun, which gives us our daylight. Of course you know this is the day that we call Sunday.

The moon reflects a pleasant light.

And the next day of the week is named for the moon, which reflects a pleasant light at night. This is Moon-day. But we spell it Monday.

4. The North Star and the Dippers

The earth spins around so that in the morning we must look toward the east to see the sun and in the evening we must look toward the west.

The moon circles around the earth so that sometimes we look toward the east, and sometimes high in the sky, and sometimes toward the west to see it.

But all night long people who live on the northern half of the earth may look north to see the North Star.

You may think of the earth as a giant spinning ball. You may call a point in the middle of the top of the ball the north pole. As the earth whirls around and around, the north pole always points toward the North Star. This is because the North Star happens to be nearly straight above the place we call the north pole. Other names for the North Star are polestar and Polaris.

The North Star is easy to find. We can always know it when we see it. We can tell where to find it because certain other stars always point to it.

There are seven stars that form a sort of star picture. There are different names for this group of stars. They are sometimes spoken of as part of the Big Bear. They are sometimes called Charles's Wain. (Wain is another name for wagon.) But, in our country, the most common name for

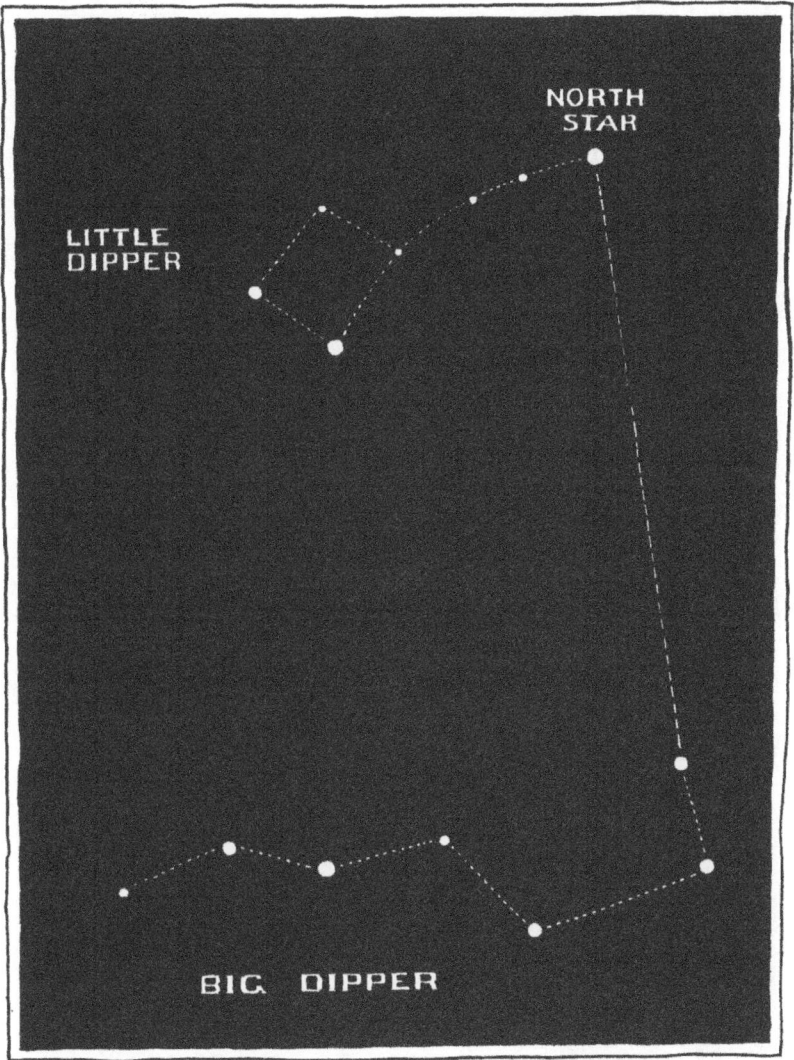

The North Star and the Dippers

the group of seven stars is the Big Dipper.

Four of the stars mark the bowl of the Big Dipper and three of the stars mark the bent handle.

The two stars in the bowl that are farthest from the handle are in a line that points to the North Star. So if you look from the star in the bottom of the bowl to the other star and then farther on in a straight line, you will see the North Star.

You can tell which way you are going any night when the stars are not hidden by clouds.

If you turn your face toward the North Star, your back is turned toward the south. Then, if you stretch out your arms, your right hand will point straight to the east and your left hand will point to the west.

Facing the North Star

So if you wish to know whether you are going north, east, south, or west, you can tell by finding the North Star.

Many people traveling on strange roads have kept from losing their way by looking at the North Star.

People walking at night where there are no roads can tell which direction to take by looking for the Big Dipper and watching the North Star. They are often glad to have so good a guide.

The North Star may guide men at sea.

Even if you are on a ship far out at sea, you can still know which way you are traveling if you can watch the North Star. Many sailors have been thankful to see it.

Sometimes we see the Big Dipper to the east of the North Star with its handle down. Sometimes we see it to the west of the North Star with its handle up. Sometimes we see it above and sometimes below this star.

But, no matter which way the Dipper seems to be tipping, it is always the same shape and the same two stars point toward the North Star.

There are seven other stars in the north which make a star picture of a dipper. We call this group of stars the Little Dipper. Four stars form the bowl of the Little Dipper and three stars form its crooked handle. The last star in the handle of the Little Dipper is the North Star.

The bowls of the two Dippers have their tops turned toward each other. So the Little Dipper looks as if it were pouring into the Big Dipper. Or the Big Dipper looks as if it were pouring into the Little Dipper.

The North Star does not shine by reflected light like our earth and our moon. It shines with its own light, as our sun does. The North Star is a sun.

All the stars in the two Dippers shine with their own light. They are all suns.

We can see thousands of stars in the sky without giving our eyes any help. If we were to look through a telescope, we might see millions more. And all these thousands and millions of stars are suns. The stars are suns and the suns are stars.

A telescope

Our sun is a star like other stars. The reason it looks larger than other stars is that it is nearer the earth than any other star.

The reason the North Star looks smaller than our sun is that it is so far, so very far away.

SCIENCE GAMES

1. The Sky at Night

Look at the sky at night. Ask some one to show you the North Star, the Big Dipper, and the Little Dipper.

1. Draw a picture to show the positions of the Big Dipper and the Little Dipper when you saw them.

Show in your picture if the Little Dipper looked as if it were pouring into the Big Dipper. Or show if the Big Dipper looked as if it were pouring into the Little Dipper.

The two stars that are farthest from the handle in the Big Dipper are called the pointers. Can you tell why?

2. Look at the moon. Draw a picture to show what shape the moon seemed to be when you saw it.

Looking through field glasses

3. Is there some one who will lend you a pair of glasses that make far things look nearer and bigger? If there is, look at the moon through such glasses.

4. Tell in what ways the moon seemed different when you used such glasses.

2. Sunlight

1. Put some peas and beans into a pot of moist soil. Keep the pot in the sunlight near a window.

Do the pea and bean plants grow well? What color are their leaves?

2. Put some peas and beans into a pot of moist soil. Keep the pot in a dark drawer or under a dark box or in some other dark place.

Do the pea and bean plants grow well? What color are their leaves?

3. Can you tell, by looking at a person's face and hands, whether he stays outdoors or indoors most of the daytime? Is his skin darker if he stays indoors almost every day?

4. How does skin become tanned?

3. Suppose

1. Suppose you could take a trip to the sun and the moon! Which place could you reach in the shorter time?

2. Suppose you could plant some seeds on the sun! They would not grow. Why not?

3. Suppose you could plant some seeds on the moon! They would not grow. Why not?

4. Suppose you were on the moon, looking at the earth! What could you see?

5. Suppose you could go for a walk on the moon! Would you see only smooth and level places? How are people able to learn about the far-away moon?

ROBERT'S SCIENCE PARTY

The day Robert was nine years old he received several presents. His mother gave him a glass prism; his father gave him a magnet; his grandmother gave him a compass; and his grandfather gave him a rubber comb, a glass rod, and a silk cloth.

Ruth came to see Robert's presents. She brought him some candy she made herself. The cousins had a good time playing with all the presents.

"Robert," said Ruth, "I wish some of our friends could play with your presents, too."

So Robert invited some boys and girls to his house for a party.

1. Prisms and White Light

A prism can be made of different things and it can be made in different shapes. Robert's prism was a glass one. It had three sides and two ends. The sides and the ends were flat and their edges were straight.

White light passing through a prism

281

The glass in the prism was not colored. It was colorless like pure water. But when sunlight passed through this glass, it shone in different colors.

The sunlight did not show these colors before it went through the prism. It was a white light, then.

White light really has different colors in it. But when they are all mixed together, they do not show.

These colors can be seen only when something breaks the rays of white light into its rays of different colors.

A glass prism can break white light into all the colors of a rainbow.

Robert covered the window to make the room dark. But he let a beam of sunlight come in through a hole in a piece of cardboard. He put the prism where the beam of white sunlight would shine through it. He had a large piece of white paper on the wall on the other side of the prism.

After the beam of white light passed through the prism it was not white any more. It had been broken into bright colored rays. The colors showed on the white paper. There were different shades of red, orange, yellow, green, blue, and violet.

Other things besides glass prisms can break white light into colors.

Did you ever take a walk early some sunny morning in summer and see the dewdrops on the grass?

Dewdrops, themselves, are colorless. But when sunlight is shining on them it is broken into its different colors. We say then that the glistening dewdrops are glittering like jewels.

Other drops of water besides dew can break white light and reflect its colors.

Look at a lawn sprinkler when the sun is shining on it some day. Turn your back toward the sun and look at the fine spray from the sprinkler. You will see colors in the spray like those of a rainbow. But the spray, itself, is colorless. The colors you see are the broken beams of white light reflected by the fine drops in the spray.

There are many ways by which

white sunlight can be broken to show its colors. The prettiest of all is the way of a rainbow.

Sometimes you can see the sun shining and rain falling at the same time. Then, if you turn your back to the sun, perhaps you will see a rainbow. The best rainbows are to be seen rather early in the morning or rather late in the afternoon, when the sun is not too high.

The sunlight touches the raindrops or mist in the air. Then the white light is broken into colors, which are reflected by the drops of water.

Perhaps you can see a wonderful great colored arch with its ends reaching the ground far away. But if you should go to the place where the ends seem to be, you would not find the rainbow there. It would still be just as far away.

So you may just as well enjoy the rainbow from one place as another. Wherever you are you can see that the outside color is red, the next color is orange, the next yellow, the next green, the next blue, and last of all is the violet on the inside.

Of course you will wonder why white sunlight is reflected with red on the outside of the rainbow and violet on the inside. And some day you can learn why this is so, if you study more about rays of light and their colors.

2. Games with Electricity

The children at Robert's party wondered what games they could play with a rubber comb and a glass rod and a silk cloth. Robert and Ruth showed them how to play games.

Robert rubbed the comb with the piece of silk. He next held his comb near bits of paper. The bits of paper moved swiftly to the comb. They clung to the comb and did not fall.

Then Ruth took the silk cloth and rubbed the glass rod with it. The glass rod could pick up bits of paper, too, after it was rubbed with silk.

After that all the boys and girls took turns playing with the rubber comb and the glass rod.

They found some pieces of cotton and linen and wool cloth. They pulled out threads and tried to pick these up with the rubber comb and the glass rod. They tried bits of hair and other fibers, too.

Sometimes the threads and paper moved very quickly to the comb and the glass rod. Sometimes they moved just as quickly the other way.

One boy said, "Let's rub other things with silk and see if they will pick up threads or paper."

Ruth wore some pretty beads. They looked like yellow glass. They were amber beads. She rubbed the amber with silk. Then she picked up bits of thin paper with her beads.

Playing with electricity

When some things are rubbed together, electricity is caused to stay on them. If glass or hard rubber or amber or many other substances are rubbed with something like silk or fur, there is enough electricity to make some things move toward them or away from them. The bits of fiber or paper are pulled or pushed by the electricity.

"Last winter I had a silk dress and a silk scarf," said one of the girls. "Sometimes, when I tried to take my scarf off, it clung to my dress. When I pulled it away there was a crackling sound. If the room was dark, I could see a little spark. Electricity made the silk scarf act that way."

"Once I rubbed my shoes on the carpet when I walked across a dark room," said Robert. "Then I touched a key with my finger. I felt electricity on my finger and I saw a spark when I touched the key."

"My hair makes a crackling sound when I comb it with a rubber comb," said Ruth. "Electricity makes my hairs fly away from one another when I use a hairbrush."

"We have a black cat at our home," said one of the boys. "Sometimes his fur crackles when I stroke it with my hand. If I stroke the fur in the dark, I often see little sparks. So I named the cat Electricity. I wish I had brought him to this party."

3. Magnet and Compass

Robert put some tacks on the table. Then he held his magnet near the tacks. The tacks jumped from the table and clung to the magnet. The tacks did not fall from the magnet. They were not shaken off.

When Robert wished to take the tacks away from the magnet, he took hold of them and pulled them off. If he let go of them, they jumped back to the magnet.

A magnet is something that has power to attract bits of iron, steel, nickel, and certain other substances.

The tacks were made of iron. Robert's magnet could attract them. It had power to make them move.

So the tacks jumped to the magnet and clung to it.

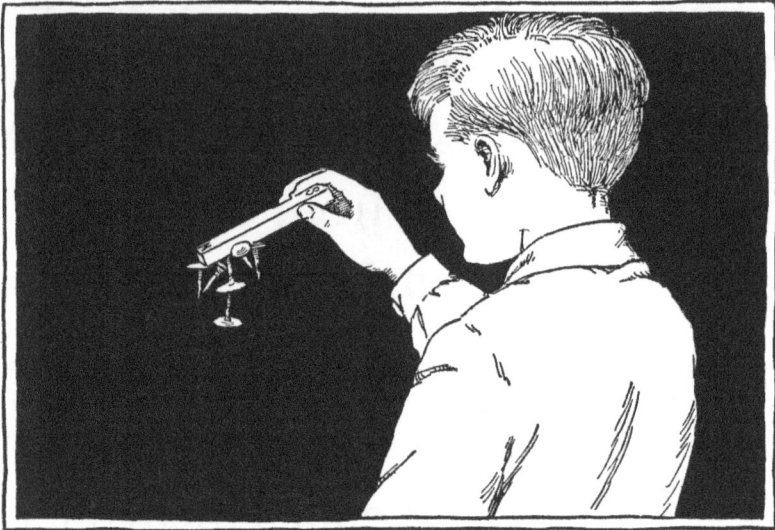

The tacks clung to the magnet.

At first Robert's magnet had been just a bar of steel. It had no power to attract bits of iron. Later it was changed to a magnet.

A steel bar or a steel needle can be changed to a magnet with electricity.

Sometimes wire is wound about a steel bar like a thread around a spool. If electricity is sent through the wire, it makes a magnet of the bar.

A piece of steel can be changed to a magnet, too, by placing it near another magnet.

People have not always known how to make magnets. The only magnets they had in early days were pieces of rock they found in the ground.

This kind of rock could attract bits of iron and certain other substances. It was called loadstone, or lodestone, and was prized very highly.

When a narrow bar or needle of lodestone was hung in the air by a thread, it swung so that one end pointed toward the north. The other end, of course, pointed southward.

If a steel magnet is straight, like a bar or needle, it will point toward the north and south, too, if it can swing. It can swing when it hangs by a thread or string tied to the middle. It can swing if it is pushed through a cork and placed in a glass of water. Or it can swing if it is made the right shape to rest and balance on a sharp point.

In some places on the earth, a magnet points exactly north. In other places it does not point straight north. But in each place it always points one way. So people can learn which way a compass points in different places on the earth.

We call a magnet a compass if it is placed so that it can swing with one end toward the north and the other end toward the south. We call one end of a compass its north pole and the other end its south pole.

People know that the sun is near the east in the morning and near the west in the evening. They know that one star, called the North Star or polestar or lodestar, is always in the north.

But some days and nights are cloudy. We cannot always see the sun or the North Star. Then it is most helpful to have a compass.

Men need compasses when they travel over land where there are no roads and no maps to guide them.

A pilot, who is the man who steers a ship, needs a compass. By looking at his compass he can tell which way to steer the ship by day or night. He can know where to go in fair weather or in storm and fog.

Do you wonder why one end of a compass points to the north?

The earth is an enormous magnet with a north magnet-pole and a south magnet-pole. These two poles are not points like the ends of a steel magnet. They are two places with great power to attract iron and some other substances.

The power of these magnet-poles is so great that they can move a small compass needle even though it is many, many miles away.

A compass

The needle does not jump all the way to one of these poles like the tacks moving to the near magnet. But it swings so that one end points to the far north pole of the great earth-magnet.

SCIENCE GAMES

1. Playing with Magnets

Ask your teacher if you may play some games with magnets at school.

1. What did the children at Robert's party do with the tacks and the magnet?

Play the same game they did.

2. If you have some steel needles that are magnets, put one through a cork and let it float in water. Then you will have a compass. Which way does your compass point?

3. Let a magnet needle hang by a thread. Which way does it point?

4. How can a compass be made so that it can be carried in one's pocket?

2. What Will Happen?

1. Find some clear glass cut in a shape that will act like a prism. What will happen if white light shines through it? Do this and see.

2. What will happen if you rub a rubber comb with a piece of silk and then hold it near bits of paper? Do this and see.

3. Place a lawn sprinkler so that the spray will be in the sunshine. What will happen when the white light of the sunshine touches the misty spray? Do this and see.

4. What may happen if you scuff across a thick carpet and then touch a door key with your finger? Do this and see.

3. Name Three Guides

Read these rhymes about three guides. Then tell their names.

Men sometimes lose their way and go
Along strange paths they do not know;
And then, at night, they look up high
And see me steadfast in the sky!

If you are lost some bright clear day
And cannot seem to find your way;
To know directions, you would best
Watch for me setting in the west!

If clouds hang heavy overhead,
And unknown ways you wish to tread;
Just look at me. Then you can tell
Which way you're going, very well!

www.ingramcontent.com/pod-product-compliance
Lightning Source LLC
Chambersburg PA
CBHW031237090426
42742CB00007B/227